the Enlightened
RELATIONSHIP

12 Proven Concepts for Creating *a Happier Relationship through Communication, Conflict Resolution, and Conscious Action*

MANDIE BIGELOW
— AND —
TOBEY BIGELOW

ISBN: 979-8-9869297-0-5

Published by T. & M. Bigelow Publishing

Contact us at https://www.facebook.com/enlightenedrelationship

CONTENTS

INTRODUCTION

Do you feel like you and your partner are speaking different languages? Are you frustrated with your communication, or lack of it, and of not feeling heard or understood? Do you frequently find yourself worrying about what your partner is doing, where they are going, or who they're talking to? Are you missing the passion you felt when your relationship was new? Or the close, loving connection you felt? Are you having the same fights over and over? Do you feel angry? Resentful? Or empty, like something is missing but you don't know what?

Even if you're not in a romantic relationship, there is likely wisdom in this book that will enrich your life. This book is written from our perspective as a couple, but the concepts and lessons we convey apply to any type of relationship.

Whether your marriage is on the brink of collapse or you've just begun a new relationship and want to know how to keep it running smooth...Whether you're sick of fighting the same fights and getting nowhere, or you feel like your efforts to love aren't felt or reciprocated...There is something in this book for you.

Why do I need it?

Relationships are hard. They do *not* work if we simply love each other. The truth is, most of us haven't been taught the skills we need to have successful relationships by our teachers or parents. We *need* solid information, like this book, that we can actually apply to make things better.

What can I get from this relationship book that I can't from others?

Many relationship books are written by one person whose perspective is from one field of study. Our book is by two people who *each* happened to study relationships from multiple, different fields of study. So, our book has insights on relationships you will not see elsewhere all in one place, including Eastern philosophy, Western psychology, metaphysics, spirituality, biology, and sociology. We then refined our most beneficial and easy-to-use findings and made this book.

You'll learn concrete conflict resolution skills so you don't have to have the same fights over and over. You'll learn what causes many conflicts so that you can greatly decrease their number. You'll learn how to communicate better so that you can get more of what you want in your relationship. You'll learn how to get more in touch with yourself so that you can prevent emotional and psychological dramas that drain energy from both you and your partner.

Who We Are

My husband and I were each on our own answer-seeking path long before we met. The relationship model we present in this book is the result of twenty years of study between the two of us on personal growth, relationships, science, spirituality, Eastern philosophy, martial arts, and psychology, with sources ranging from books to workshops, teachers, mentors, and real-life experiences. Our work has been refined and worked into a functioning model for an honest, loving, respectful, fun, spontaneous, and ever-growing relationship. We tried to pack all of the most helpful, life-changing ideas and tools we've found into this book.

This book is designed to provide couples with tools, concepts, tips, and tricks we use to:

1. Maximize our ability to work as a team to effectively deal with anything from minor irritations to relationship-threatening issues

2. Increase time spent enjoying each other's company

3. Increase our ability to learn from challenges and grow closer as a couple

4. Deepen our self-awareness and understanding of universal truths that are at the core of our struggles

Brief Overview of the Benefits You'll Get

Benefits of our relationship model:

1. I really feel like we're a team. We each make the other's life easier. We work together to get stuff done. It feels great knowing there's someone who has your back and is there to help you out when you're in a jam.

2. We don't get stuck in conflict-induced bad moods for extended periods of time because we make our relationship's well-being a priority. We take time to work stuff out as it comes up. We don't just give each other the cold shoulder for days, purposely avoid dealing with conflict, or pretend things are fine when they're not.

3. So, we have more time to enjoy life together and grow together.

4. We feel we can trust each other because we both do our best to be transparent.

5. We feel valued and appreciated by each other, because we make an effort to show and communicate it.

6. We both have better health.

What is an Enlightened Relationship?

To understand what our idea of an enlightened relationship *is,* it's important to note what it is *not:*

1. People who have "mastered" how to be happy and at peace

2. People who act kind and loving to each other all the time

3. People who are perfect and don't need to work on themselves or their relationship

4. People who communicate flawlessly

5. People who always sacrifice their needs for their partner

6. People who have the same exact life views

7. People who have never done illegal or immoral things in their pasts

8. People who are in the relationship only for sex, appearance, status, money, or to "fix" or "rescue" their partner

Now, what *is* an Enlightened Relationship? Here are the five key elements that lay the foundation:

1. What do we mean, exactly, by the word *enlightened*?

The word "enlightened" means *aware, awake,* or *conscious,* and that is what we mean in this instance. The true core of an enlightened relationship is *awareness* and *acting on purpose.* When we say "aware," we mean "seeing" what's going on with yourself, your partner, and your relationship. Both parties do not necessarily need to be fully self-aware, but they need to at least be working on it.

So many of us function unconsciously. When we're not self-aware, we act out relationship-destroying behavior patterns we observed our parents or guardians performing when we were in childhood. I remember when I acted unconsciously, not having any clue why I was acting the way I was, why I felt the ways I did, and feeling powerless to stop my actions that were hurting my partner. It's easy to play victim and blame our parents for why we struggle to have healthy relationships, but the truth is, we're perfectly capable of taking responsibility to change that.

2. You *want* each other. You don't *need* each other.

> *"The purpose of relationship is not to have another who might complete you, but to have another with whom you might share your completeness."*

> – Neale Donald Walsch

There is a common view in our society that our perfect partner will "complete us." That they make us whole, they are our other half, they make us happy, or they make our life worth living. This is garbage. Once we give someone else responsibility for our happiness, stability, and fulfillment, we give ourselves permission to blame them for our unhappiness and dissatisfaction as a result. In an enlightened relationship, both individuals recognize that they are responsible for their own happiness and fulfillment. They do not enter a relationship to fill some hole in themselves, but because they enjoy being with the other person. They recognize that they are already whole themselves, so instead of putting energy into getting love and attention from each other, they can put their energy into lifting each other up. Fortunately, we both entered into our relationship understanding this idea. We enjoyed each other's company and wanted to share fun times and adventures. We had already each done enough work on ourselves that we didn't *need* each other to feel good.

3. It's not perfect, but it's real

Contrary to what you might think, an enlightened relationship is not a smooth-sailing, happy-all-the-time kind of relationship. The ideal relationship is not perfect, but rather, both parties make the best of what they have, work together to overcome challenges, and do things that say, "I love you, and I support you," every day. They make mistakes. They fight and yell sometimes. But they say, "I am sorry, and I am not proud of the way I handled that or how I treated you." They take what they can from the hard times as lessons to aid them in the next challenge they face.

The arguably most enlightened person on earth agrees: The Dalai Lama himself said, it's not that he is always happy—he sometimes feels sad, scared, or angry, just like the rest of us. It's how you handle those emotions that matters, not whether or not they are there.

4. Honesty and transparency *aren't* overrated

An enlightened relationship is based on trust. In order to have that, both parties need to be honest and transparent with each other. They share their fears and their dreams. They share their feelings and opinions. They each strive to stand up for what's important to them, even if it's not popular in the other's eyes. They say what they mean and speak up if they're not happy.

We didn't always have trust in our relationship. We had to work through some major trust issues early on. I didn't understand why keeping things from each other, even if seemingly insignificant, could cause damage. But if you lie or hide the truth about one thing, your partner has no way of knowing what else you'd be willing to lie about. It can be really, *really* hard to build trust back after it's broken, and you won't always succeed. But we decided that being together was worth the pain and struggle of rebuilding trust again, so we put in the work to repair it.

In our society, dishonesty in relationships is not only common, it is also accepted, and in some cases even encouraged. It's "normal" to keep secrets, to gossip behind your partner's back, to keep things from each other to get something you want or avoid something you don't want. Should anyone be surprised that so many people are struggling with insecurity, jealousy, resentment, fighting, breakups/divorce, court, and lawyers?

We do not feel safe, we do not feel trusted, we do not feel like we can count on our partner to have our backs, we do not feel loved or respected. And yet, many of us would do ANYTHING to avoid the vulnerability of opening up and exposing our true feelings, desires, and our deepest fears. But if we did, we would find that the kind of security we long for in our relationship is finally possible.

5. Basic respect, teamwork, and responsibility

Both parties need to treat each other with respect. It may seem obvious, but the importance of this is sadly overlooked. We're not just talking about men treating women with respect here, either; women need to treat men with respect as well (more on why this is so important to a happy relationship in a future chapter).

An enlightened relationship also requires teamwork, and sometimes giving up a certain degree of rigidity or stubbornness. Both people can't always get their way. Sometimes, they need to make sacrifices and compromises for the greater good of their future together.

When the relationship is going through a tough time, both parties don't try to hurt each other and blame each other for everything going wrong. Instead, they try to focus on what they really want (to find answers, solutions, and get back to being happy and feeling connected again). They work as a team and take responsibility for their part in things. They know that when they hurt each other, nobody wins.

At its core, the goal of an enlightened relationship is to help people move away from acting out unconscious, destructive patterns and toward living and acting on purpose. Now, let's get into the details of how we make our relationship work!

Chapter One

Awareness Is the Beginning of All Growth

"Life is a great school and nature is the ultimate teacher. But without awareness or fee attention you won't hear the teacher or learn the lessons of nature. Awareness transforms life experience into wisdom and confusion into clarity. Awareness is the beginning of all growth."

– Way of the Peaceful Warrior

We believe most relationship problems are caused by unconscious behavior patterns, which we *can't* change unless we're aware of them. If issues like lying, cheating, insecurity, emotional dramas like jealousy, communication breakdowns, and power struggles thrive in your relationship, the first step to change is to start observing yourself so you can find out what your patterns are. It's easy to have trust issues in your relationship if, for example, in your communication with each other, you're not aware you're being dishonest. Another example would be, when your fears come up and you're not aware of them, you may do whatever it takes to make you feel safe, even if it's not a wise or logical decision. This could be saying you're fine when you're upset to avoid confrontation, or leaving out certain facts and embellishing others to get your partner's praise, respect, or

approval. You do not need to be good at being aware, but you need to commit to working on it.

Most importantly, self-awareness gives you the ability to *choose* how you treat the person you love and be the person you want to be.

It also helps you:

1. Understand yourself better

2. Understand your relationship better

3. Learn more about yourself and your relationship

4. Work through issues faster and more effectively

5. Learn from your challenges

6. Stop repeating your destructive patterns

7. Grow closer as a couple

8. Heal old wounds

9. Feel happier and more fulfilled

10. Not get blindsided by serious problems in your relationship

Self-awareness is developed by learning and observing. You'll notice the things you learned about as they show up, if you're paying attention, and the more you observe yourself, the more useful information you can gather and the more you'll be able to understand. If you don't practice paying attention to yourself, you'll continue to repeat your destructive patterns. If you do the

work and discover your patterns, however, you'll have a baseline to work from and a better idea of how to get to where you want to be. There's no point in focusing on changing your partner if you want to resolve issues in your relationship. You cannot control anyone else, so the change must start with you.

Self-awareness isn't easy

I won't sugarcoat it; looking in the mirror can be hard. It can feel like the bad kind of hard, not the good kind. Some people are afraid to admit weakness in certain areas because they think it means they are unworthy, a failure, not good enough, etc. We all have shortcomings. It doesn't mean they're our fault, and it also doesn't do any good to beat ourselves up over them.

Things to observe:

Your thoughts

Your thoughts affect your emotions, your emotions affect your actions, and your actions affect the quality of your life and your relationship.

Everyone has their own unique way of interpreting the world around them. Everyone also has their own way of interpreting themselves. When we are very young, as we begin to learn language, we begin to form our own schemas (ways of seeing the world). We adopt many of the things we hear people say about us as the ultimate truth, without ever questioning these beliefs.

The self-image we create sometimes has nothing to do with our true nature. However, the effects of who and what we believe ourselves to be and what we believe we are capable of are the

difference between a happy, successful person who's comfortable in their own skin and someone who's likely involved in one criminal offense after the next, and who's depressed and angry at the world.

IF YOU DO NOT LOVE YOURSELF, NOTHING ELSE MATTERS. Stick a sign on your fridge, tattoo it on your arm, I don't care. Do whatever you need to do to remember this.

That's right—if you do not love yourself, it doesn't matter how loving your partner is to you. It doesn't matter how rich, how smart, how compassionate, how loyal, or how dedicated they are to you. You still will not feel loved enough. If you have beliefs like *I'm not good enough*, *Nobody cares about me*, *I can't measure up*, or *I'm a failure*, it's not going to matter what your partner says or does. You will hear and see what confirms your beliefs about yourself in their words, body language, and actions. And you will be wrong. Your partner will tell you they love you and you'll hear it but won't believe it.

Your Emotions

Your emotions are a great tool, if handled appropriately, for guiding you toward further growth, fulfillment, and happiness in your relationship. Especially the not-so-pleasant ones.

Your actions/behavior

How are you treating your partner? In what areas can you improve? There are probably plenty of behaviors you're unaware of that are making your relationship harder than it has to be. Working on finding these destructive behaviors and replacing them with

actions that secure trust, support, and intimacy is a very powerful way to create change in your relationship.

Key takeaways

1) Awareness transforms our experiences into wisdom and confusion into clarity.

2) You need to be willing to look at yourself objectively and admit the part you're playing in your relationship's problems.

3) We need self-awareness for growth and change to be possible in our relationship because we're starting with what we *can* control—ourselves.

4) Problems in relationships are often due to unconscious behavior patterns, which we can learn to stop doing once we become aware of them.

5) Looking in the mirror can be hard, and not beating yourself up when you start seeing things you don't like can be hard as well. You have to remember to be kind to yourself and keep going.

6) The three things you want to pay attention to are 1) your thoughts, 2) your emotions, and 3) your behavior.

Chapter Two

YOUR RELATIONSHIP IS NOT A LEAN-TO

"We can complain that rose bushes have thorns, or rejoice because thorn bushes have roses."

– Abraham Lincoln

"When we are no longer able to change a situation, we are challenged to change ourselves."

– Viktor E. Frankl, *Man's Search for Meaning*

Why do we find ourselves suffering and hurting in relationships where we were once high as a bird in the sky, happier than we ever thought we could possibly be? Or why are we constantly flip-flopping between the highs and the lows? Why do we feel like a victim to all the stuff our partner puts us through?

Because we've become dependent on our partner for our happiness. We came to the false conclusion that our partner makes us happy in the falling-in-love stage of our relationship. We became dependent on getting their attention and love, and then when things got challenging, or boring, or our partner's behavior failed to meet our expectations…we became hurt and upset.

16

We forgot, or never knew, that we had the ability to make ourselves happy, so we blamed our partner for failing us. Our partner can certainly influence our happiness, but we are ultimately responsible for it.

Where's the proof that we determine our own happiness?

There are plenty of people with disabilities, life-threatening diseases, or who are poor as dirt who are happy. There are plenty of people who are millionaires, have loving friends and families, or are perfectly healthy but are depressed. Happiness is not circumstantial. It is all what you do in your mind that determines your emotional well-being. This proves that the source of our happiness is NOT coming from the outside—not from money, our partner, our job, or our living environment—it's coming from within. We both agree, however, that external things do influence our state. Some things are more difficult for us to deal with than others, because of our beliefs, experiences, etc.

Love is like a drug

The Celestine Prophecy, one of the main books that guide our relationship's philosophy, talks about this. It says that we are all perfectly capable of generating our own love and happiness. We can all connect with the universal energy in various ways, the energy referred to as God, Love, the Holy Spirit, the Divine, and other names. When we fall in love and our partner gives us lots of attention, affection, appreciation, and respect, it fills us up with this energy and feels so good. Just like a drug, we can become addicted to receiving love from our partner, and we mistakenly believe that this is the *only* way we can get it.

Need versus Want

My husband and I had each learned about this before we got together. When we got together, we talked about how we wanted

to *want* each other, not *need* each other. We knew that to have a healthy relationship, we couldn't use each other to fill voids we felt in ourselves. Do you think you might *need* your partner? Answer these questions:

a) Do you only feel worth something when engaging with them?

b) Do you only feel valued when engaging with them?

c) Do you only feel accepted when engaging with them?

d) Do you feel an emptiness inside when they're not present?

e) Do you get angry easily with them?

f) Do you feel hurt often by them?

g) Do they or you think you "overreact" to things?

If any of these are true, you may be depending on your partner for your happiness. This doesn't mean you don't love them and care about them. It means you either forgot how to make your own happiness, or you never learned how to do it consciously.

Because your thoughts affect your emotional state, it may seem like certain things really do *make* you happy. But it is actually your mind *interpreting* everything you encounter outside of yourself. In other words, it is what you think *about* things and the *meaning* you put on them that determines how you feel.

Expectations

In one of Tobey's martial arts classes, he explained how having expectations can get you killed in a real-life fight. Less extreme but still important, having expectations about your relationship will lead to unhappiness.

What happens next is, we start *expecting* to get that good energy from our partner. We *expect* them to act certain ways, say certain things, and do certain things that we feel lift us up. We think these things are "good." We like them. We think that's how our relationship "should" be.

But sooner or later, our partner won't do or say or act in one of these certain ways, or they'll be in a bad mood, and suddenly, we're screwed! We think these things are "bad." We don't like them. We want our partner to stop doing things that "make" us feel upset and start "making" us feel good again! We forget that we have a car and money and are perfectly capable of going to the store and getting our own damn happiness.

One of our favorite books, *Way of the Peaceful Warrior* by Dan Millman, says it this way: "If you don't get what you want, you suffer; if you get what you don't want, you suffer; even when you get exactly what you want, you still suffer because you can't hold on to it forever."

When we depend on our partner for happiness, we feel disempowered, scared, stuck, and frustrated. Our partner feels pressured, taken for granted, frustrated, and not free to be themselves. When we think our partner causes our happiness, how can we not *also* think they cause our *un*happiness?

When we want a certain outcome, like for our partner to respond to us in a certain way when we are expressing emotions, we set ourselves up to be miserable. We only get hung up on wanting a certain outcome when we place value judgments on things that happen in life. When we get so hung up on what could be, we struggle to cope with what is. We make life so much harder than it needs to be. We make ourselves suffer. When we think this way,

we open up the flood gates for stress, disappointment, anger, and grief.

When you have expectations, *you lose both ways*:

Have you ever had an expectation for a situation to go a certain way and then it didn't? Of course, you have—we all have. What happened? You were disappointed, of course. Did you ever consider the possibility that while you were busy having a bad attitude about things not going the way you wanted, you might have missed something even greater than your expectation?

When your expectation WAS met:

Say you expected to have an awesome birthday party. You did, therefore your expectation was met. But what happens when that birthday party ends? How do you feel? You think you will be happy as long as your expectations are met, but you won't because nothing ever stays the same. You get what you want, but you can't hold onto it forever.

Have you heard the saying, "fitting a square peg in a round hole"? Having expectations is like that. It will be harder to flow with life. You will be dissatisfied because whatever does meet your expectations won't last, and whatever doesn't will make you unhappy.

We will be more upset when something happens in direct opposition to what we decided was our preferred outcome. When we think, *If this is the way it turns out, I will be happiest*, and then exactly the opposite of that happens, we are more upset. Whatever happens to you is for you. Even if you have no clue how what has happened is what is best for you, trust that it is somehow.

Summary

If you were hoping we were going to teach you the secrets of how to get your partner to do what you want, you can put this book down now. Unless you take responsibility for your happiness, certain problems will likely follow you for the rest of your life, no matter how much your partner changes, or even if you change partners, make more money, or buy a new house. When you take responsibility for your happiness, you stop being a victim. You worry less about what your partner is going to say or do because you know that your happiness doesn't depend on them. Knowing that happiness comes from within ourselves, and not falling victim to the belief that we "get" our love and happiness from our partner, is one of our relationship's building blocks. We must feel we are complete—or good enough—by ourselves, not like we need our partner to "complete us."

Chapter Three

THERE ARE NO PROBLEMS - ONLY OPPORTUNITIES TO LEARN AND GROW

"The problem is not a problem, your attitude about the problem is the problem."

– Way of the Peaceful Warrior

"When it rains it pours. Maybe the art of life is to convert tough times into great experiences. We can choose to hate the rain or dance in it."

– John F. Marques

There are so many different methods out there for dealing with the issues that inevitably come up in intimate relationships. But have you ever stopped to consider, *maybe issues aren't actually bad*?

Most people see issues as bad. But issues in relationships are chances for improvement in disguise.

This philosophy is another cornerstone of our relationship. Like we explained in the last chapter, perspective is a powerful thing. Sometimes, what you need is not to find a solution to your

problem, as much as you need to change your perspective about the problem. When you see it as a challenge that offers opportunity for things to be even better, the problem ceases to be a problem.

Issues don't mean you're in the wrong relationship

The idea that good relationships have no difficulties is a myth. If you believe this, you could miss out on an incredible relationship. You and your partner are totally different people, raised with different belief systems, with different brain chemistry, and different perceptions of the world. It would be crazy to expect no conflict. It's your differences that make you intrigued by one another, keep your relationship interesting, and make you potentially better together than alone. Healthy relationships have difficulties which are worked through together for continuous growth and improvement. (Of course, everyone has their limits. Sometimes, we may feel that whatever difficulties we face aren't worth staying in the relationship. Only you can make the call of what's right for you.)

We need the change and growth. We don't learn the most when things are going smoothly; we learn the most when they're not. Most people feel unhappy in relationships which have become routine, boring, and stagnant. Would you agree that the more knowledge and awareness you have, the easier it is to adjust and improve your relationship? If you answer yes, you can probably see how challenging situations can be useful to the long-term health of your relationship.

If we view challenges as "issues," it's hard to find solutions

When we fixate on something that scares us, our body reacts to what's happening in our brain. Most people have heard of the fight-or-flight response, when stress hormones flood your body and make you ready to fight or run away. Your blood pressure and

heart rate rise as well. But this is the thing people don't always place as much importance on as we feel it deserves: What happens to your mind. The more your stress goes up, the less you can think clearly and be rational. And the less you can think clearly and rationally, the harder it is to find solutions. It is also much harder to communicate.

Of course, when issues come up, they can feel very overwhelming. They can feel very unwelcome. You just want to go back to that blissful feeling that you had before. But on some level, you are ready for the growth; otherwise, it would not be there. When you're struggling with an issue, ask yourself, "What is this situation trying to show me? What can I learn from this?" This signals to your mind that you are willing to receive insight. It might not come right away. Just keep asking. And don't question the thoughts that come to you about it. Don't try to logic it out.

If thoughts about the issue have come to you but you still feel unclear, tap into your feelings. Notice how your body reacts to your thoughts. Does it tense up anywhere? Do you feel uneasy? These thoughts are not the truth. Does your body relax? Do you feel peaceful or a tiny bit excited? Then these are the thoughts you want to listen to. We all have this inner wisdom available to us, but we have to open ourselves up to hear it.

These examples show how a "Problems" mindset can make you stuck and miserable, and an "Opportunities" mindset can create growth, problem-solving, and more connection with our partner.

Situation:

One person has trust issues from previous relationship experiences, and they are affecting their current relationship, even though there has been no reason NOT to trust the current partner.

View 1:

This isn't fair, this puts us at odds with one another, you should just trust me, you should be more understanding of why I don't, etc.

View 2:

This isn't a great situation, but it doesn't spell the end of our relationship unless we let it. What can we do about it? How can I help you trust me more? How can I be more trusting? How can we work together to make a plan to bring us closer to where we want to be? Maybe we can use this as an opportunity to become better teammates. Maybe we can learn what works and what doesn't and be better prepared for dealing with issues in the future.

Situation:

You are both in financial straits. You're both stressed because it's been getting harder and harder to afford the cost of living. You don't think you can make rent this month and the car needs to go to the mechanic. Neither of you seem to be able to make enough money and you both work a lot already.

View 1:

This is a big problem. What if we get evicted, or one of us loses our job because we can't get to work? We're burnt out, angry that all our hard work seems to get us nowhere, and afraid of what our future holds. We don't know what to do.

View 2:

We are both unhappy living this way. What can we do about it? Let's use this as an opportunity to improve our money-managing

skills, our time-management skills, and reassess our values and priorities when it comes to spending. Let's take this opportunity to connect with the community for side work or combine our creativity to find ways to generate extra income.

In the "Problems" examples, we need to point out that **there's nothing wrong with acknowledging the things you're unhappy about or afraid of. The key is to not get stuck there**, and to move on to looking for opportunities.

When we're in a tough spot, we can ask ourselves questions like these to cultivate a "No Problems" mindset:

Could this be an opportunity for me to…?

Learn something new?

Get better at something?

Grow closer to my partner?

Go for my dreams?

Overcome a fear?

Grow and mature as a person?

These questions can help you shift your focus from seeing problems to seeing opportunities. If you remember that there are no problems—only opportunities to learn and grow—you'll gain competence in handling challenges in your relationship. You'll also get better at handling ones outside your relationship that you face with your partner. And with the experience, you'll gain confidence in yourself and you'll be less overwhelmed when challenges arise.

RELATIONSHIP

Summary

If we can see the challenges in our relationship as opportunities instead of problems, we'll have a relationship that is a lot more enjoyable, with a lot less struggle. Challenges don't mean your relationship is bad or wrong, necessarily. The idea that good relationships should have no difficulties is a myth.

If we see challenges as problems, our ability to find solutions decreases. It's okay to acknowledge when things are difficult. The key is to not get stuck there.

Chapter Four

WHY IS COMMUNICATION SO HARD?

"The difference between the right word and the almost right word is the difference between lightning and a lightning bug."

– Mark Twain

I'm sure you've heard about how important good communication is for your relationship's success, but what you might not know is *exactly* what "good communication" means. Couples need communication concepts they can understand, and concrete skills they can learn to use whenever they need them. The tips we give here are the ones we use over and over with success. Tobey and I both studied communication in depth, so this chapter really dives deep into why communication is so hard, exactly how it fails us, and how to fix it.

You can't have an intimate, evolving, happy relationship without good communication. Without good communication you may…

1. Feel like you and your partner are speaking different languages

2. Not feel heard or supported

3. Feel unappreciated

4. Feel unloved

5. Feel disrespected

6. Feel frustrated and distant

7. Feel alone

8. Have the same arguments over and over

9. Frequently hurt each other emotionally

To communicate, you first need to encode your thoughts and feelings into language you think will be comprehensible, then you send your message. The message your partner *hears* is not necessarily the message you tried to send. Your partner has their own unique way of perceiving the world and has to decode your language into what he or she believes is the meaning. This diagram, from the book *Parent Effectiveness Training* by Dr. Thomas Gordon, illustrates just how complex communication is:

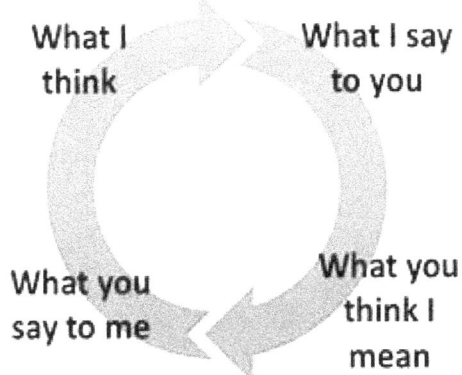

Reference: Gordon Model http://tinyurl.com/mgk469l

RELATIONSHIP

Communication is not simply what you say and what you hear. You are conveying opinions, thoughts, desires, ideas, not just with which words you choose to use, but also with your silence and where and how you use it. You also convey yourself with body language, tone of voice, volume and speed of your speaking, and expression. Even more subtle, but still picked up by your partner even if only on a subconscious level, is the energy you are giving off. Are you upset but saying you're not? Your tone, posture, and facial expression will give off a different energy, and your partner won't be fooled if what you're saying doesn't match.

Why Our Communication Fails

1. We don't communicate

2. We're not honest

3. We hear what's not there and don't hear what is.

4. The *way* we communicate

1. We don't communicate

Often, the biggest problem couples have with communication is simply that they are not communicating enough. Have you ever gotten mad at your partner because it seemed so obvious that they were going to do something, and yet, they didn't? Have you ever ended up in an argument because one or both of you made an assumption? Have you or your partner ever felt disrespected for the other one making a decision that affected you both without talking about it? This doesn't mean you have to tell your partner every passing feeling or darkest thought you've ever had; there's a balance to find, just like with everything else. However, not discussing issues won't make the issue go away. When one person

holds onto negative feelings about their partner without talking about what's bothering them or resolving it within themselves, the issue will eat at them until they blow up at the next little thing that goes sideways.

Here are some guidelines for when it's appropriate to communicate in a successful relationship:

1. When there is a conflict.

2. When you have strong feelings that are influencing the way you interact with your partner.

3. For ANY decision making that affects both of you.

4. When you are unhappy with an aspect of your relationship.

If it affects your partner, discuss it.

Some of us think communicating is just common sense, but we still don't do it. Why? Fear is a big reason. You will be afraid if you want something but think you might not get it. Humans are driven by two things: to seek pleasure and avoid pain. This applies here. You might have something you want but are afraid that if you speak up about it, you might not get it. You might be afraid of rejection, criticism, or conflict. You might not actually feel what one would describe as *scared*, you may just feel a little tense or nervous. This is a clue to check in with yourself and find out what you want or don't want, what you are thinking, and if your actions line up with what you believe is the right thing to do. You might wholeheartedly agree that you should speak up when what you want affects your partner, but if you are not functioning from a mindset of seeing the big picture, your desire will dictate your actions.

Saying you want something, prefer something, or would enjoy something gives your partner more information for how to love you. They want you to be happy! If neither of you know much about what each other's desires and interests and preferences are, how well do you think you can make each other happy? In addition to saying what you want, things will work better for you if you're also willing to compromise and not have an attitude if things don't always go your way. This works fine if you're invested in your partner being happy as well.

Another reason you may not communicate as much as you should is because of beliefs such as this: *If he really knew me, he'd know what I was thinking.* Or, *If she paid attention, she'd know what I need.* Do these beliefs really hold up when you look at them critically? Even if he does know you well, does he always know what you're thinking? Of course not! Maybe she would have a better understanding of what you need if she paid better attention, but can she always know? There are a thousand different variables that affect what you need in any given situation. Some of which, neither of you may be aware of.

If there's a chance talking to your partner may make your life a lot easier, or avoid a misunderstanding or an argument, why pass it up? What would you gain? And what's the worst that can happen if you make an effort to consistently talk to your partner as honestly as you can? You will either make it easier for your partner to love you and show you that they care and respect you like they *want* to do, or they won't like what they hear, and the two of you may realize that you are as not as compatible as you first thought. If you do go your separate ways, you open yourself up to being with someone who aligns better with who you really are.

The more aware of your desires, fears, and thoughts you are, the easier it is to make your actions conscious. If you don't even

realize you have this desire to avoid conflict, or a fear that you can't get what you want if you speak up, how can you watch out for what you say and how you say it?

Unspoken Requests

An unspoken request is a term we coined for when we want something from our partner but we do not ask. We may hint at it, but we do not communicate it directly. Then, we get upset when they do not do what we wanted. We justify to ourselves why they *should* understand what we want, and if it mattered to them, they would do it! (Women tend to fall into this trap more than men. When I don't want to directly ask for something, it tends to be because I want to avoid feeling selfish or appearing needy.) We forget that with our vague hinting, it may seem obvious to *us* what we want our partner to do to show love and support, but that doesn't mean it's obvious to *them*!

2. We're not honest

Honesty is such an important concept in an enlightened relationship that we dedicated a whole chapter for it. See chapter six.

3. We hear what's not there and don't hear what is

Another reason our communication fails: we incorrectly interpret the messages we hear from one another. We hear the incoming message through our own unique, personal filtration system of our beliefs, values, opinions, and experiences. We make assumptions about our partner's intent and meaning based on our perception without even being aware we are doing it. The expectation that you

can learn to know exactly what the meaning behind your partner's message is 100 percent of the time is ridiculous, even if they are *always* honest.

Why? Because each of us has our own unique pair of lenses through which we perceive the world. Not just over our eyes—all of our senses are affected. The lens is our mind. All the experiences we take in filter through our minds. We have our experiences, and we have what we think *about* these experiences. This is why, often, two people who witnessed the same event will tell different stories. You could say the same things that drove your last partner up the wall and they won't faze your current partner at all.

So, even if your partner is honest and direct with you, the line of communication can still get screwy if your filter is adding false information to the mix. Your partner can say something with a caring intent, but if her tone or word choice reminds you of your mother or previous partners trying to control you, you may take offense.

Being open, honest, and direct to your partner is NOT being undermined. This alone will drastically improve your communication and trust. But being aware of your mind's influence on what you hear is equally important. We dedicate an entire section of this book to discuss how the lens of our mind can negatively impact our relationship and what we can do about it.

Language accuracy

Another reason our communication fails is lack of language accuracy, which we cover in depth in chapter nine, "Conflict Resolution."

Summary

Communication is so hard because we each have our own unique filters that the information we hear has to pass through. Our communication fails because of not being accurate with our language, not being honest, not speaking up when we should, misperceiving or making assumptions about what we hear, or because of *how* we communicate (tone of voice, body language, etc.).

Chapter Five

HONESTY

"My past conduct was so transparent and so honest that when my enemies spread rumors about me nobody believed them."

– Amit Kalantri

Having honest communication is one of the largest rocks in our relationship's foundation, but that doesn't mean we always had it. In fact, I sucked at honest communication in the beginning of our relationship, and we went through a challenging time to rebuild broken trust. Honest communication, partnered with an effort to truly listen to each other, allows us to resolve sticking points in our relationship, overcome fears and insecurities, make plans, compromise without struggle, and help each other feel loved and fulfilled. We do our best to be honest, transparent, and not hold back things we're afraid our partner might not like or agree with. We let each other in when we're struggling, and we always try to express our truths.

Without honest communication, your partner may end up surprising you years down the road with an I'm-not-happy-and-want-out-of-this-relationship you never saw coming. You can't both be happy long-term. If you're not telling each other what you like and don't like, you're not giving each other information

needed on how to be supportive and increase your partner's quality of life. You'll also have to deal with failed expectations.

Trust and security

Not communicating with honesty will eventually lead to a breakdown in trust. This can be very difficult to come back from, and many couples don't have the level of commitment, investment, and patience it takes to repair the damage. Recovering from broken trust can be done, however. We know this from personal experience. When you don't know for sure if your partner has your back, and you can't believe anything your partner says, you can't count on them and you can't feel safe in the relationship. A person afraid to trust is afraid of being hurt. To feel protected from pain, they'll close themselves off emotionally and mentally from their partner. Instead of having an intimate connection, both parties will struggle to connect and feel close.

When a person is dishonest in a relationship, their partner can feel stressed about what they're saying, doing, where they're going, who they're texting. The person who's stressed will ask a lot of questions and may come across as controlling and smothering. The person being questioned will feel doubted or smothered or controlled and will possibly become resentful toward their partner, and thus, a wedge is driven between the partners.

Inner Peace

How does being honest bring you more inner peace?

Because you'll have less conflict between your thoughts and your actions and words.

Inner peace creates a less drama-filled relationship. How?

Because it is the conflicts already in you which are projected onto the relationship.

Self-worth issues:

Self-worth issues can cause much drama when they are projected on the relationship. From our experience, some of the negative self-perceptions can be caused at least in part from the inner conflict that comes from not being honest. We learned that low self-worth can be improved if honesty is practiced. It is as if when you are dishonest, a part of you knows it, and uses it as more fuel for you to not like yourself.

New Relationships

In the beginning of a relationship, each person presents the highest version of their self to the other. They are accepting, forgiving, considerate, and loving. They overlook each other's weaknesses for the most part, or those they notice are outweighed a hundredfold by their strengths and amazing qualities. Both feel loved and free to love; they feel no need to keep the energy for themselves.

It's important to acknowledge that, although we all have the potential to be this way, it is not human to function from this state all the time. If you expect your partner to function from their highest potential all the time, you will be disappointed. No one is perfect. Someone may be good at something that you are not, but you will be good at something else that boggles their mind. We are all growing, and all have our own weaknesses and challenges to work on.

When a person feels they have a good grasp on who they are, are okay with that person, and have a handle on how to be the person

they want to be, there will be less of a gap between the version they present in a new relationship and the place they live from most of the time. Consequently, when a person has less awareness of who they are and less of a grasp on how to live as the person they want to be, the gap between their highest version and where they are most of the time will be bigger. **Stick to your values.** Don't lie about your values or preferences to "win" his or her approval. If you lie about who you really are or what you believe in, the truth will eventually come out and/or you'll be unhappy. If you're not compatible, it's best to know up front so you can handle it.

We can be unknowingly dishonest

Dishonesty in our communication is a pattern some of us have developed to do one of two things: Feel good or avoid feeling bad.

As human beings, one could argue that we are all selfish. We all like to feel appreciated, valued, and accepted. We don't like to feel rejected, ignored, or taken for granted. Some of us place a higher value on what others (especially loved ones) think of us than we do on being honest. Think of a child wanting to hide something they did that they know was naughty from their mother or father because they don't want to be scolded. Or of a child embellishing a story to make themselves appear more like a hero to hear their parents' praise. Many of us still function this way as adults. For example, we hold back telling our partner the truth of what we did if we think our partner will be upset. We fear feeling rejected by our partner's reaction.

Dishonesty in communication may not seem obvious. This is because 1) we use other methods than outright lying, and 2) we developed this way of communicating when we were kids and it has become second nature/subconscious. Here are two more subtle ways we're being dishonest:

1) Leaving things out. We think, *But I'm honest about what I say*...The truth is, by leaving out facts and details that matter in your communication, it's easy to convey a meaning quite different than the truth.

2) Twisting facts. We put more importance on some details and less on others by the way we phrase things. It may be surprising that such an intricate process can happen subconsciously, but we know from experience that it can.

Leaving information out, or twisting the facts, has the same effect on your relationship as outright lying.

You have to be aware of yourself to be honest

Those of us who are good at lying are experts at lying to ourselves. We justify anything we need to in order to feel good about ourselves. And if we can convince ourselves that we are either not lying or that the lie is necessary, or of the rightness of our lie, then we do not even know our communication is destructive to our relationship. Like most things in this book, transforming dishonesty into honesty starts with self-awareness.

"To share your weakness is to make yourself vulnerable; to make yourself vulnerable is to show your strength."

– Criss Jami

Be honest, especially when it's not easy or convenient

It's important to try to be honest with everything, but it's the times that being honest scares us the most that *have the biggest impact on the quality of our relationship*. There is *absolutely no point* in being honest only when it's easy or it serves you. The added bonus

of being honest when it's the hardest to is, if you're trying to change a pattern, this is the fastest route.

Be honest with yourself about yourself, with yourself about your partner, with your partner about yourself, and with your partner about your partner.

Each of these aspects is important to consider and here's why:

1) Be honest with yourself about yourself.

If you're not honest with yourself about yourself, then you can't be honest with your partner. For example, you've convinced yourself that you don't care about how your partner acts around his or her friends. You tell yourself, "As long as they love me, that's all that counts," but deep down, you feel not right inside. If your partner asks what's up when you seem to have an attitude about how they've been acting with their friends, you can't be honest and say it bothers you because you're trying to convince yourself that it doesn't.

2) Be honest with yourself about your partner.

Oh boy. Many of us can relate to *not* doing this. The old phrase "blinded by love" certainly holds merit. Blinding ourselves to the truth of our partner can be downright dangerous. For example, you begin to get sign after sign that your partner is just plain crazy. You ignore them. You decide to leave your friends and family and move in with your partner in another state. Your partner links your bank accounts and drains all your money, and before you realize it, you're stranded with no one else to turn to and no money to get home.

"Hiding how you really feel and trying to make everyone else happy doesn't make you nice, it just makes you a liar."

– Jenny O'Connell, *The Book of Luke*

41

3) Be honest with your partner about yourself.

This is especially a problem in the early stages of relationships. *If you're not honest in the beginning, you're setting your relationship up to fail.*

It's easy to get swept up in the thrill and bliss of a new relationship, but it's important to remember that if you are looking to give it its best chance of success, you need a strong foundation. You don't have to know if he/she is "the one" before you commit to giving your best to the relationship. You can't ever know the future of the relationship. You can't know whether you will enjoy a lifetime of love and companionship or an intense couple of months where you learn a meaningful lesson and move on. Don't look for a guarantee of outcome before showing up fully, with transparency and honesty, not hiding your weaknesses to impress or pretending to share his interests when you don't to be liked and accepted. If you do not fully show yourself, you may never see your partnership's potential.

I learned this lesson the hard way. When I started my second relationship, I held back things about myself that I feared would bring up concerns for compatibility and potential value conflicts. I had learned how to lie to myself and others and was well practiced at this. Without being aware of what I was doing at the time, I put a lot of effort into making myself appear easy going, likeable, and like the perfect partner.

However, I fell completely in love. We shared so many passions, life goals, and values. I was disbelieving, in awe, and high in the clouds. The only problem was: he was living his values; I was not. I was apparently unaware that I hadn't yet learned how to apply the ideas of the kind of person I wanted to be. When the truth came out after months that I wasn't living the ideas I said mattered most

to me, in one second, our relationship went from perfect bliss to *can we make it work at all?*

We both decided our relationship was worth the fight, and we put our all into making our relationship be the way we perceived it was in the beginning. It took patience, persistence, faith, and acceptance, but we got there. I learned that if you try your best to be completely honest from the beginning, you save yourself and your partner a lot of struggle! And if you're not honest, you're setting the relationship up to fail.

We have this illusion that we will be more liked and therefore happier if we appear to the world to be "better" people than we currently are. (That may be more successful in our career, more selfless, richer, more liked by others, depending on our own definition of "better.") We love to portray ourselves as happier, smarter, more giving, tougher, more easy-going than we are in truth. On the surface, this seems to "work," meaning we may get more attention and affection for a time. But in a committed relationship, sooner or later, your partner will see the inconsistencies in your actions, your not-so-pleasant side, and your shortcomings. They may feel misled, made a fool of, or lied to, which will cause a lot of strain and/or end the relationship.

If you are willing to feel vulnerable and expose your true self honestly in the beginning of the getting-to-know-each-other stage, then what kind of partner do you think you've found if they see your shortcomings and decide to give a go at a relationship with you regardless? It's easy to want to give your all for someone's ideal vision of themselves that they're projecting, but it takes true strength of character to decide to give your all when you see the best and the worst of someone else.

4) Be honest with your partner about your partner.

It's probably self-explanatory why it's helpful to be honest with your partner *about* your partner when discussing things that concern them. But in case you need it, here's an example of how things can go sideways if you're not: Your partner is contemplating taking a new job. They ask you if you think it's a good idea. Based on what you know about your partner, you don't think their personality and talents would fit the new position well and would be better suited elsewhere. But not wanting to crush your partner's confidence, you say you think it's a great idea. Your partner takes the job and gets let go in a month because of the reasons you thought wouldn't make them a good fit, and they have to start the job search again.

Another thing we strongly recommend NOT doing if you're unhappy with your partner is *complain about them behind their back*. This breeds insecurity and distrust in the relationship, doesn't fix anything, and may put unasked-for advice in your head, which could create more problems if you act on it. Most likely, this person you vent to is close to you. Naturally, they care about you and don't like hearing you be unhappy. They have only heard your side, and they are biased toward you. They naturally want to blame your partner for you being unhappy, when in reality, you may well have caused the problem. Instead of helping you cultivate the attitude of partnership and camaraderie between you and your partner, they may encourage pitting you against one another. Not because they don't mean well but because they care about you. Complaining about your partner behind their back opens the door to distrust, resentment, and insecurity problems, and doesn't solve anything. If you have a problem with your partner's behavior, have the balls and the respect to tell them to their face.

How to improve honesty

1) Pay attention to yourself inside

What things/situations/feelings do you want? What motivates you to do what you do?

What things/situations/feelings do you fear or want to avoid?

What's motivating you to be dishonest? Is it a specific fear? Is it a belief like, "Being honest isn't really that important"? Or, "I won't get what I want if I'm honest"? Or, "I'll be taken advantage of if I'm honest"?

Are any of the above beliefs true?

2) Pay attention to what comes out of your mouth

Does what you say line up with what's going on inside?

3) Reprogram your brain and your responses

Pay attention to find the times you're most likely to choose dishonesty.

Use those times as an opportunity to choose honesty instead.

If you mess up, you can still apologize and tell your partner the truth later.

4) You can't be honest 100 percent of the time; what matters is that you try

5) Things to keep in mind when you're improving your honesty

a. Expect yourself to mess up

b. Don't EVER believe that you've gone back to square one

c. Don't mentally punish yourself when you mess up

d. Don't give up on changing a dishonesty habit; it can happen faster than you might think

e. Expect to feel uncomfortable and vulnerable; this will change with practice

The best way to change a dishonesty habit is to practice being honest in situations you feel uncomfortable in, and repeatedly experience an outcome other than the one you fear.

Summary

The biggest problem with dishonesty is that it breaks trust, which not all people are able to recover from. Lack of trust in each other makes it impossible to have a close relationship where both people feel secure. In addition to causing rifts in relationships, being dishonest can also cause or contribute to self-worth issues and inner turmoil. How honest we are when starting a new relationship can determine whether or not that relationship succeeds or fails. When it is difficult to be honest is when it's most important to do so. Humans function to avoid pain or gain pleasure, and being dishonest is one way we manipulate other people's behavior to get the results we want. We can be unaware of our own dishonesty, and if we generally feel insecure, being dishonest can be our standard behavior method in relationships. If you want to change a dishonesty habit, you must become aware of yourself, then practice, expect to make mistakes, own up to them, expect to feel vulnerable and uncomfortable, but keep going!

Chapter Six

THE ALIEN

"Nothing can hurt you unless you give it the power to do so."

– A Course in Miracles

All of us have an alien living in our heads. The alien is the little voice that makes us afraid, insecure, and distrusting. It strips you of your joy, confidence, and hope and makes you afraid to trust—in yourself, in your partner, and in life. Scientists refer to it as the subconscious, but it has been studied throughout history and has many other names as well. It's like a young child, driven by the need to feel loved, safe, accepted, and approved of, and doing what it can to avoid pain and rejection without considering the bigger picture of how the ways it chooses to meet these needs will impact itself and others in the long run.

The alien is trying to protect us from getting hurt. Although his intentions are good, his advice is not based in truth or reality. And if we believe him, it does us more harm than good. We can feel awful about ourselves, avoid pursuing our dreams, resist trusting our partner and letting love in, etc.

He says things to you like, "Better not do that…You're gonna fail," and "You're such a loser, you'll never be good enough," or, "She

doesn't really care about you, she's gonna break your heart," and "His friends are more important to him than you are." (The alien represents fear, yes, but we are not saying that fear is something you should never listen to. If you were standing at the edge of a cliff and you didn't feel afraid or ignored the feeling, then the likelihood of you falling would increase because you would not conduct yourself as cautiously. The kind of fear the mind produces that we call "the alien" is an irrational fear that does NOT benefit you to adopt as truth.)

"FEAR is an acronym in the English language for 'False Evidence Appearing Real.'"

– Neale Donald Walsch

The alien seems adept at blowing things out of proportion, finding false evidence to support his opinions and making it seem real, and not being able to see the big picture or anything that opposes his views.

The Sphere

When you and your partner are having a conflict and the alien begins to influence one or both of your thinking, unpleasant emotions begin to rise. As the alien takes over your mind, fear takes over your body. Directly proportional to what you're thinking, your body responds physiologically, and your ability to see options for handling the situation diminishes. Your heart rate rises, stress a.k.a. fight-or-flight hormones flood your system, muscles clench, and rational thought (to some degree or another) flies out the window.

The inner circle contains the options you see when your body is functioning in fight-or-flight mode. The outer circle contains

examples of ways you can see to handle the situation more productively. When in fight-or-flight mode, your scope of awareness closes down to tunnel vision, but if you can keep your cool when things get challenging, your scope of awareness doesn't get as narrow and you can access the options in the outer circle. Resolving conflicts will be easier and won't result in regrets and hurt feelings.

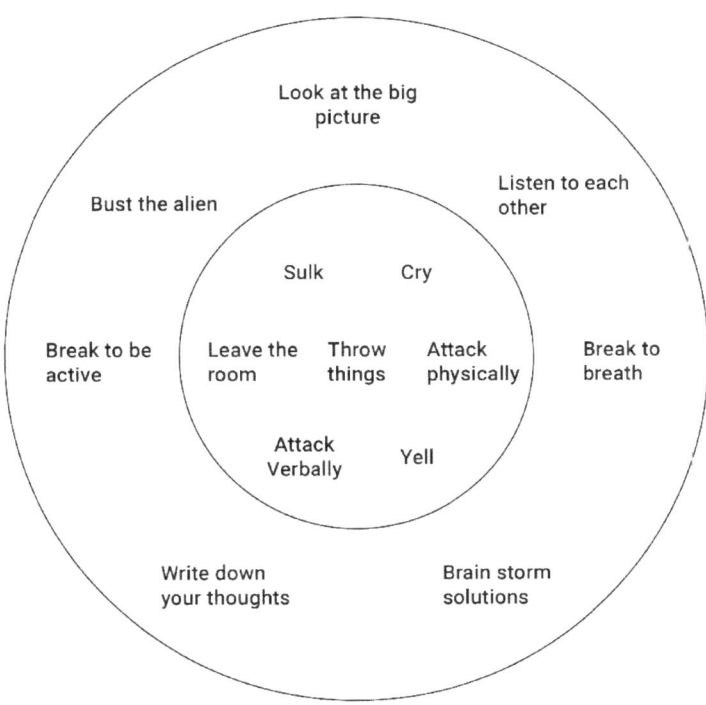

Your Alien's Blinders

Like a horse wearing blinders, when you believe your alien, you put blinders on your perception. Communication between you and

your partner can be challenging enough normally. Throw the alien into the mix and it won't matter if your partner is *crystal clear* with what they say—if your partner's message contradicts what you're believing in that moment, your brain will change the meaning of their words to match what's true for you.

This is a known phenomenon that psychologists call a "schema." A schema is basically a mental framework we use to interpret information. We like things to be organized and to make sense. Information that corroborates our current beliefs, we accept; information that contradicts our current beliefs, we reject.

If your alien likes to whisper, "You can never be good enough," your partner may tell you that they enjoyed something you did for them, intending to convey appreciation and nurture your understanding of each other for a stronger relationship, but you won't see that because your alien has blinders on you. You won't see their true intention if you're buying in to the bullshit. It will appear to you that your partner is sending the message that all the other times you didn't do this thing, they were disappointed in you, and you aren't good enough.

Self-Worth and the Alien

Low self-worth is connected directly to the alien lie that makes you doubt how much your partner cares about you.

If we don't believe we are good enough or worthy or deserve to be treated with respect, then we may take any number of things our partner says, does, doesn't say, or doesn't do as evidence to support our belief.

You may not be aware your alien is affecting you, but if you notice that specific "doesn't care" thought regularly, that's a clue that YOUR alien is sabotaging you and your relationship.

Make sure you discuss the times you had these thoughts with your partner to find out if you were making false assumptions. Hear their side. They likely came across uncaring when they were distracted, had their own alien talking, when they were exhausted, or any number of other possibilities.

Try not to take everything personally. Try to have a base assumption that your partner DOES care about you, if you have to assume something. It would be more realistic. They are in a relationship with you, after all.

The Big Picture

Another way to say, "Look at the big picture," is to say, "Put things in perspective." Imagine looking at your partner though an empty cardboard tube, but all you can see is one little stain on their shirt. It's irritating the heck out of you. But when you put the cardboard tube down, you see your whole partner, the room, and everything around them. One little stain doesn't seem so irritating anymore. You might realize that your partner was wearing the stained shirt on purpose because they were doing home repairs. Looking at the big picture helps reduce the number of clashes we have with our partner. And when we are trying to resolve a conflict, especially when our alien and emotions get in play, combating tunnel focus with the big picture will make it easier to resolve one efficiently and effectively. You spend less time being stuck and more time growing in your relationship.

It's helpful to keep the big picture in mind anytime we're acting from a not-so-good place, be it confusion, uneasiness, fear, guilt, anger, self-pity, helplessness, etc. If you're human (without any serious empathy-lacking psychological disorders), you've had at least one experience where you've said or done something to someone when you were upset that you later regretted.

Remembering the big picture when emotions are running rampant can greatly reduce unnecessary hurt in your relationship.

How do I "look at the big picture"?

Ask yourself questions:

Will the impacts of my actions be *for* or *against* my values?

What is really important to me? Or, what are my values?

What other factors might be in play that I haven't accounted for?

How might my words or actions impact my relationship, my partner, or myself?

How well does this choice reflect the person I want to be?

Is this the person I want to project into the world?

What are all possible consequences of this choice?

Do I want to take the risk of one or more of those things happening?

If I hurt my partner with the means of feeling better myself, how good do I really feel?

Am I treating my partner like my enemy or like they're on my side?

"When the mind resists life, thoughts arise. When something happens to conflict with a belief, turmoil is set up. Thought is an unconscious reaction to life...When you resist what happens, your mind begins to race; the same thoughts that impinge upon you are actually created by you."

– Dan Millman, *Way of the Peaceful Warrior*

Living with Your Alien

Viewing your alien as the enemy only gives him more power. How? Imagine you are thinking thoughts like, "Oh my god, it's my alien again! I hate him! He's ruining my life!" Now, how do you feel? Confident? Accepting? At peace?

Resisting your alien puts you in a distraught emotional state. You are still on your alien's turf. He is still running the show. How do you get out of this? As with everything else, there is no one right way, but here are the two main ideas we have found helpful:

1. See your alien with a new perspective.

Try to remind yourself that your alien is trying to protect you and it is the only way he knows how. He just can't see the big picture.

2. Bust your alien.

We have had great success with this "alien-busting" technique together. It gives your partner an opportunity to work with you as a teammate instead of feeling like you have turned them into the enemy (which can easily happen when you listen to your alien). Busting isn't the same as fighting your alien, although it may sound similar. Think of it as debunking, or disproving, what your alien is saying by bringing into focus the bigger picture and the higher truths. Try to acknowledge that what your alien is saying may not be the truth, without getting yourself into a fearful or angry emotional state over it.

With practice paying attention to your thoughts, it will get easier to identify times when your alien is taking over. If you are aware of it, it is easier to not give him power by saying to yourself, "I know this is my alien, and I can't see the big picture or even the

truth right now." If you can't find the truth and bust the alien on your own, ask your partner for help.

Stress, Heart Rate, and the Alien

1. Stress affects the way our bodies work.

The more we worry, stress, and try to control, the more out of whack our bodies get and the more on edge we become. Physiologically, we are more prone to jumping to negative conclusions and not seeing the big picture.

2. Scientists have discovered that, depending on the state we're in, the electromagnetic frequencies of our heart and brain can either match up or be out of sync. When we're stressed, scared, or angry, our heart rate increases, hormones and chemicals are released and created to prepare us to fight or run (fight-or-flight response), and the frequencies get out of sync with the mind.

3. We have something called heart intelligence. When the heart and mind frequencies are out of sync, we have trouble seeing the truth, being rational, and knowing what we need to do to help ourselves. It's like intuition, guiding us all the time.

4. We can purposely calm ourselves by breathing slowly and relaxing, thus letting our heart rate calm down so it becomes easier to hear our inner guidance system.

5. We will not be able to calm down if we stay in our head, listening to our alien. That's why it helps to do things like relax our body or focus on our breathing, on our heart, or on any of our senses, like beautiful things we see, how our body feels, what we

taste, smell, or hear (like listening to music). We come out of our head, back into our body and into the present.

Additional tips for dealing with the Alien:

1. Pay attention to your emotional state and what's going on in your mind.

2. Don't fight how you feel (it is not "bad" to feel negative emotions).

3. Don't have the expectation that you can "get rid of" your alien.

Try to accept that your alien will always be living with you, but you can learn to not listen.

Remember that when you are upset or afraid, you are resisting life, your thoughts, or what is.

4. Look for fear. Ask yourself what you are most afraid of, or what's the worst that can happen.

5. If you don't know what your alien is saying but can identify what you're feeling, try asking, "If this feeling had a voice, it would be saying…"

6. Bust the alien. Once you've brought to light your alien's fear, ask, "Is it true?" Seek the truth. Apply the "Big Picture" mindset by finding examples of situations and facts that show you why it's crazy to believe your alien.

7. If you're having trouble finding perspective, ask your partner if they'd be willing to help.

8. Change your physical state. You can do things like breathing exercises or taking a walk to help you see more clearly as well.

Alien Lies to Watch Out For

He/she doesn't care

I'm a failure

I'm not good enough for him/her

I'm not important to him/her

I'm a loser

I'm not smart

I'm not good at _____

He/she is gonna leave me

He/she doesn't value what I want

He/she doesn't value my opinions

(Jealousy and paranoia alien lies can also be from low self-worth. If you don't think highly of yourself, you'll doubt how much your partner values the relationship.)

Summary

The "alien" refers to the thoughts and belief systems we all have based in fear, doubt, and insecurity. Like a small child, our aliens are trying to keep us safe. The alien is very good at gathering evidence to "prove" to us why we should heed his warnings. If we believe him, however, it can sabotage our relationships and our

lives. We can deal with the alien by proving him wrong (dispelling the false beliefs), putting things in perspective by looking at the big picture, and reassuring him. The alien will be there no matter what, but only when we believe him will it cause struggle.

IF *you believe the alien, it can…*

Sabotage your happiness

Drive a wedge between you and your partner

Make you feel stressed or have anxiety

Make communication with your partner extremely difficult, increasing the number of misunderstandings or fights

Make you repeat behavior patterns that are destructive to your relationship and personal happiness and growth

If you don't believe the alien, you can…

Have less emotional drama in your relationship

Resolve conflicts more efficiently

Not feel like victims of energy- and intimacy-draining patterns

Feel confident and happy being yourselves

Experience each other's love more fully and freely

Chapter Seven

TEAMWORK

We like to think of our relationship as a team because it makes life easier and we're both happier. Here are our top tips for making that idea a reality:

The best thing you can do to be a good teammate is be the best version of yourself you can be.

As we talked about in the previous chapter regarding taking responsibility for your happiness, keeping your energy up will make it so that you're not depending on getting it from your partner. You'll be less prone to taking offense at things and getting into petty arguments if you're in a good place.

Act from an "us" attitude, not an "all about me" attitude and not an "all about you" attitude.

To act from an "us" attitude means you take your partner, yourself, and your relationship into account in the everyday decisions that you make. For example, your son from a past relationship wants to sleep over at your house, which you share with your current partner. If you were just thinking about yourself, and you wanted him to, you'd agree to the sleepover plan. If you were only concerned with your partner being happy, you might decline. But

with an "us" attitude, you'd consider the impacts on both of you, and would likely go talk it over with your partner.

An "all about me" attitude means caring more about getting what *you* want than you do about you *both* being happy. For example, you really want to go to your friend's party at a time you and your partner usually do something. You know your partner doesn't like this friend, and you figure they won't want to go. But instead of talking to your partner about it to see if you can come up with a compromise, you just go and don't tell them. You think, *I really want to go to this party, so they can suck it up!* When your partner finds out, they feel like you didn't acknowledge that you normally spend that time together. They feel hurt and feel that if you had told them you really wanted to go, they probably would have been okay with going for a little while. But now they're upset, so you get into an argument, and you don't end up having fun at the party anyway because of it. Do you think your partner will feel more inclined to respect what you want if you respect what they want? Or do you think they'll feel inclined to respect what you want if you act like you don't care about what they want?

Why we are sometimes selfish can be because we're afraid we won't get what we want.

We mistakenly believe that if we're considerate of our partner's needs and desires, they'll take advantage to get more of what they want, regardless of what we want. In most cases, however, your partner is in a relationship with you because they care about you. If your partner doesn't care about you, you may want to ask yourself why you're staying with them. Considering your partner's needs and desires is more likely to inspire reciprocation rather than you getting gypped.

An **"all about you" attitude** means caring more about your *partner* getting what *they* want than you do about you both being happy. For example, your partner likes to stay up late and watch TV with you. You would rather go to bed earlier, but you want them to be happy, so you stay up. You don't tell your partner what you want, but the next day, you're tired and cranky.

It's not a problem to sometimes sacrifice what you want for what your partner wants. It's a problem when you always do it.

If you always make sure your partner is happy but neglect yourself, you'll eventually end up bitter and resentful. In a healthy relationship, the sacrificing goes both ways. People who are all about making their partner happy tend to not say what they want much, or say they don't care, or they're fine either way. If you really are easy going, that is also not a problem—it's when you *do* have an opinion and you're not *saying* it.

When the self-sacrificing partner ends up bitter, the other person will be taken completely off guard because their partner was quiet about their unhappiness for weeks, months, or years.

Fight from an "us" attitude, not a "me against you" attitude.

Why some couples have such a hard time with disagreements is because they forget that they are on the same side. They forget sometimes that trying to come out on top, or ahead, or better, or smarter than your partner doesn't lead to a happy relationship. If either person tries to win, you both lose. When the winner wins by putting their partner down, the "loser" will feel hurt and may withhold love or emotional connection or "get back at" the winner later. It may seem childish, but many adults behave this way when they're in an intimate relationship.

What do you do instead?

If you're going to fight, fight for what you both really want: To resolve your conflict, to understand each other, to find the truth, and to feel safe, happy, and at peace in one another's company.

Ask yourselves what those things are, and try to remember you're on the same side.

Integrity

Having integrity means you do your best to keep your words and actions true to your morals and values.

Do you want your partner to trust you and be able to count on you? Then having integrity matters. Some adults today weren't raised to understand the importance of values such as integrity. Some think of values like this as old-school, and not having much place in today's society. Some think integrity matters but were never taught how to actually live it.

If you do this, you'll show your partner that they can count on you, trust you, and respect you. If you don't have integrity, you'll show your partner that they can't count on you, they can't trust you, and they may lose respect for you. An example of a lack of integrity: You promise your partner that next time you're upset and it has to do with your relationship, you'll talk about it with him or her. But then, when the time comes, you think, *I don't want to bother him/her with this issue*, and you say nothing. Another example of not having integrity: You talk about how important being yourself is, or being genuine, but when you feel unsure about how your partner may handle your true feelings about something, you don't open up and share how you feel.

Does it seem hard to have integrity? It certainly can be. Here's a trick that makes having integrity a lot easier:

Don't make a promise if there's ANY chance you can't keep it.

Only promise something you can control. Promises are made with the best intentions, but often people don't think about how many variables in being able to keep that promise are out of their control. If you must promise something, promise to do your best—if you mean it. Don't promise a certain outcome to a situation. Another problem with this is we can't know that the outcome we're promising is really what's best for our partner and ourselves.

Whatever your values are, live them on purpose. We share the values we live in our relationship, but we're not saying you have to have this value and not that value. The most important thing is living your values on purpose. This book is called The Enlightened Relationship for a reason. Be aware of what exactly your values are and why, and be aware of whether or not you're living them.

Support

Like we talked about in "You are responsible for your happiness," you don't want to *need* your partner's support. When a person needs their partner's support fifty times a day, their partner can feel smothered, exhausted, and like they need space.

The irony is that the more you feel you need your partner's support, the more you tend to push them away.

You'll get less support than if you hadn't been so needy in the first place. Neither of you are likely superhuman. You aren't always in a place to be supportive when your partner wants support. That's why it's good to be able to handle it yourself if you need to. If you

tend to lean toward being too needy for your partner to handle, reread the last chapter.

If you tend to be too independent, ask your partner if they'd be happier if you let them give you more support. People usually like to feel like they are contributing. My husband and I both play basketball, and we both know how irritating it feels to be on a team with someone with an ego who wants to make all the baskets single-handedly. They don't let you be part of the team—they don't let you make a difference. You feel useless and dejected.

People feel good when they can make someone else's life better in a tangible way. Relationships work flourish when both parties are giving each other something.

If one party doesn't want anything from the other, how do you think the other might feel? Don't be that guy or girl with the ego on the basketball team in your relationship. Let your partner be your teammate.

Try to find a balance between being overly needy of support and overly independent.

Kinds of support

Here are a few main kinds of support:

1. Physical

2. Emotional

3. Mental

An example of physical support may be helping with chores, errands, paying bills, planning ahead to make busy days go

smoothly, physically being there for your partner, and physical touch.

Emotional support would be treating your partner in ways that make handling emotions or emotional experiences easier for them.

And mental support would be helping your partner through mental hang-ups from past experiences, helping your partner feel safe and have peace of mind within the relationship.

Do you need more support?

First, is there anything you feel you're wanting but not getting? Exactly what kind of support is that? It may be one of the above, a kind we overlooked, or some combination.

Second, is it something you need from your partner? Or is it something you can easily work out on your own?

Do you feel comfortable asking your partner for support? If not, you may just need some practice.

Does your teammate need more support?

Here's the secret trick to finding out: Ask them! And be prepared to listen if they say they do.

Dependency

Don't become dependent on each other's skill sets.

This can be a tricky balancing act for many couples. Everyone has things they're good at and things they're not. And often, couples—especially married ones—fall into roles of certain tasks. He always takes care of the finances, and she always takes care of the

household chores. We've found that taking care of the tasks we're good at works perfectly well. We only want to warn about *not knowing how* to do the things your partner regularly handles. Because if one of you is sick, or injured, or for whatever reason can't do the jobs they normally do, you don't want to be helpless. At least know where else you can turn for help if you don't learn your partner's skill sets yourself. You don't have to be as good as your partner at what they do, but learn the basics and you won't be overwhelmed if there's a time you need to have your partner's back and keep things running for both of you. Learning each other's skill sets will also help you each appreciate how the other contributes more.

Summary:

Be the best version of yourself you can be.

Do whatever you need to do to keep your energy up.

Act from an "us" attitude, not a "me" or "you" attitude. Make decisions that affect both of you together, and if you can't, think about how your choices will affect them. Too selfish is bad for your relationship, but also being too self*less* is unhealthy.

Fight for you both to be happy, not for a winner and a loser.

Be willing to compromise if it is best for you both in the long run

Don't become dependent on your partner's skill sets.

Practice asking for support and *receiving support.*

Have integrity so that your partner can count on you.

Chapter Eight

RESPECT YOUR DIFFERENCES

"No one ever does anything inappropriate given their model of the world."

– Neale Donald Walsch

"You do not get respectful treatment by demanding it. You get it by treating yourself and your partner with respect."

– Mandie Bigelow

How are men and women different?

Most men's and women's brains are biologically different. Because of this, we think differently, have different basic values, and communicate differently. It's not as much the differences that make communication so difficult, but that we haven't been educated about it and act like it's not the case. Our communication would drastically improve if men stopped assuming women think and communicate like men, and if women stopped assuming men think and communicate like women.

Biologically

1. Brain Function

There is plenty of scientific research proving that the male and female brains are biologically different. Many people today accept

this as fact. There will always be exceptions, but we are speaking about most men and most women. Many experts would agree that the male brain tends to function more analytically, is great at compartmentalizing, problem solving, and is better at not letting emotions influence decision making in critical situations. The female brain, however, tends to be more in touch with emotions, which helps them take care of others. Dating back to our ancient hunter-gatherer days, these differences aided in our survival. A woman needed to be in tune with emotions to be a good nurturer and caretaker. A man needed to be able to stay logical and set his fear aside to protect and provide for his family.

In these aspects, some stereotypes are true.

2. Motives for communication

Communicating with our partner can be a lot easier if we have some insight into each other's motives on a very basic biological level. Again, speaking generally, men's motives for communicating are:

1) To provide and gather information

2) To solve problems

When in a relationship, both of these relate to how to provide and protect their loved one.

Women's motives for communicating are:

1) To provide or attain mental or emotional connection

2) To provide or attain comfort and security

3. Ways of Communicating

When communicating, most men tend to be straightforward. They don't like to add extra babble and fluff to the info they're trying to convey. They don't tend to talk just for the sake of talking as much as women do. They tend to say what they mean, and mean what they say. If they want a cup of coffee, they say they want a cup of coffee.

With men's primary motivations for communication being to provide and gather information and solve problems, this makes sense.

In contrast, most women will be much less predictable in communication. Women communicate to connect with one another and often do just talk for the sake of talking. Therefore, it doesn't matter to them if they add in babble and fluff. Sometimes, they mean what they say and say what they mean, and sometimes they don't. If they want a cup of coffee, they might say, "I'm tired," or, "I just smelled coffee and it smelled so good," and hope their partner gets them a cup of coffee. Sometimes, she'll say one thing and later that day say the opposite because she's in a different mood, because women state how they feel as if it is fact.

Women run into problems when they expect men to communicate like them. "Wait, I thought you said _____ because you meant _____!" Guy, "Um, why would I do that? I said____ because I meant _____."

Men run into problems when they expect women to communicate like them. "Why did you not just say that's what you wanted if that's what you wanted!" Or, "You want to go to the movies? I

thought you just said you hate the movies." Girl, "I was in a bad mood." Guy, "I can't figure you out!"

4. Coping with Emotion

When trying to cope with emotion, many women want to talk about it, and many men just want space and a bit of time to mull things over. Not ALL women are like this, and not ALL men, but even if your situation is the opposite, you can apply this awareness.

Women sometimes make the mistake of trying to make a man talk when he seems upset. They think it will make him feel better because this is what women do with other women. Many women, when they're upset, are hoping that their man will come over and try to get them to talk about it. To them, it is a caring gesture. But when a woman tries to get a man to talk about emotions before he's ready to, he can feel pressured and even less comfortable opening up. What a woman can do to be supportive is 1) ask if he wants to talk, 2) be respectful if he doesn't, and 3) let him know she's there for him.

A mistake guys sometimes make when a woman seems upset is NOT trying to get her to talk. They may think that if she's not talking about it, then she doesn't w*ant* to be talking about it, and they give her space out of respect for her. What happens sometimes is she feels like he is not being there for her, like he doesn't care, or is ignoring her when she's upset and feels extra desire for attention. A guy can help her feel more loved and supported if he asks her if she wants to talk, then dares to be persistent if she's reluctant. Ideally, a woman can make her guy's life a hell of a lot easier if she explains to him what makes her feel supported when she's upset. The same goes for guys. But we've learned what great

mental clarity we have when we're upset. It's not easy for most people to talk rationally while upset, and when we're not upset, we forget.

How to Treat Your Man

Men file for divorce less often than women do. According to marriage therapists ("7 Reasons Men Leave Their Marriages, According to Marriage Therapists" huffpost.com), the top reasons men file for divorce are 1) he doesn't feel appreciated, 2) at odds over spending, 3) someone cheated, 4) grew apart from spouse, 5) he feels inadequate, 6) lack of sex life, 7) needs not being recognized or validated.

That should give you a clue to what is important to him! Guys don't typically need a lot to be happy in a relationship. He wants to feel like you enjoy doing things with him, or just enjoy him being around, and he wants to feel like you admire the man that he is, that you have his back, and that you treat him decently, with respect, trust, approval, and appreciation.

If you are afraid of the consequences of treating your man this way, you may fear, 1) that you will lose *his* respect, 2) that you will be taken advantage of, and 3) that you will appear weak.

You think you have to fight and be strong and prove that you are no one to mess with so that you will get the respect and love you deserve. Being strong is a good thing, but when your desire to prove this comes out in things like frequently advising your man on what to do, making a fuss when he "screws up," and criticizing anything about him you feel is "not good" in the hopes that he will be motivated to change, he will feel like he can't ever be good enough to make you happy and either disengage from you or become resentful and retaliate.

He will not feel motivated to be the best version of him he can be for you. He will feel like a failure. If you treat your man with respect, trust, admiration, and approval, he will feel motivated to go to the ends of the earth for you. He will genuinely feel the desire to make you smile, make you feel cherished, and fight to the death for you if need be. You can be a mirror reflecting back to him the great man that he is. He sometimes loses sight of that man, he sometimes does things that aren't in alignment with his ideal version of himself, but trust that he can find his way back again and again because that great man is always there inside.

The impossible fight to win respect when you don't respect yourself

When one has no self-respect, he or she will seek getting it from somewhere else. The less one has for him or herself, the more they'll feel they need to get it from someone else. But since they do not understand respect, they will try to get it *not* by respecting others but by trying to control or intimidate them. Which, of course, backfires because who wants to give someone respect when they're being an asshole? So, in return, the person trying to get the respect often gets treated *dis*respectfully, likely feeling even worse and trying even harder (and therefore even less effectively) to get it from others.

Ways Women Unknowingly Disrespect Men:

Interrupting

Correcting

Telling him what he should do

Telling him what to do

Minimizing his values and concerns

Making decisions that affect him without discussion

Nagging

Trying to change him

Blowing off something you said you would do for no particular reason

Lying and leaving out information to make yourself look better

Trying to get him to talk when he doesn't want to

Always needing to be in control and not giving his leadership skills a chance

Complaining about what he does or doesn't do (This doesn't motivate him. It makes him feel like, *If I can't make her happy, why try?*)

Giving him the cold shoulder or snapping at him because you are upset but haven't told him why

What to do Instead

Listen with your full attention and wait until he pauses to say your part.

Don't correct him unless it REALLY matters. Do you know for sure you are right and he is not? And does it matter?

Ask, if you have a request.

Try to understand his point of view, and try to be understanding of the things that matter to him.

If a decision will affect him, talk to him first.

Focus on improving yourself and being grateful for what he brings into your life.

Respect his space. What makes you think you know better what he needs?

Practice being patient and having faith.

Incredible things can happen when you let go of control. Give it a try. If things go "badly" based on your view of good and bad, is it really the end of the world?

Appreciate all he does do, and all the effort he puts in to make you happy. Tell him what specifically is meaningful to you and why.

Tell him what's bothering you. Set down your shield. Set down your need to punish him for something he may or may not have even done to you. Do you think anyone deserves this kind of treatment when they may not even know what they did to upset you? In most cases, they aren't even aware they upset you.

How to Treat Your Woman

According to the National Center for Health Statistics, women file for divorce two-thirds of the time. When the couple is college educated, the woman files 90 percent of the time.

The top ten reasons women file for divorce, according to a Pennsylvania State University study:

1) Infidelity

2) Incompatible

3) Drinking/Drug use

4) Grew apart

5) Personality problems

6) Lack of communication

7) Physical or mental abuse

8) Loss of love

9) Not meeting family obligations

10) Employment problems

Get better at emotions.

Learn to identify feelings—your own *and* hers. Learn to articulate feelings—your own *and* hers. You will be able to relate to her better and she will feel closer to you (more connected to you).

If you notice she seems stressed, ask if you can help somehow.

Imagine your partner doesn't comprehend that saying something hurtful will make you sad, or that reacting non-plussed when you tell them something exciting can kill your excitement. It would be very frustrating to not relate on an emotional level. And difficult to communicate. Think Sheldon from *The Big Bang Theory*.

Learn the difference between emotional communication and logical communication.

For example: When she talks to you about making plans, that's logical communication. When she's talking about how frustrated she is with a friend, or that she got passed up for the promotion she was hoping for, that's emotional communication. When she's talking about something upsetting to her, you may hear that she's not sounding rational, and be tempted to steer her toward the logic you see she's lacking. You see she has a problem, and you want to

fix it. She may just want someone who will listen and not tell her she's wrong for feeling how she feels.

You have good intentions. Why, then, does this dynamic of conversation so often lead couples to arguments? Because when she's talking to you about something upsetting to her, she often wants emotional support and connection, *not solutions to her problems.* There will be times she is looking for help finding solutions, however, so you can always ask or encourage her to key you in on the kind of support she's looking for.

The other aspect that can lead to arguments when she's upset and you try to lead her to logic is telling her she shouldn't feel how she feels. Many guys may already know from experience that this is a **VERY BAD IDEA.** You are seeing the logic, and that feeling so upset about it isn't necessary of helpful, but if she's seeking emotional support, she only feels like you're saying she's wrong to feel how she feels. She doesn't feel like you can relate, she doesn't feel supported, and she doesn't feel connected to you.

(You've probably heard jokes about how you shouldn't tell a woman she shouldn't be upset because you'll piss her off. There's truth to that, as usual. When you say anything like, "You don't need to be angry…Cheer up—it doesn't matter…You'll be fine…Don't worry about it…It doesn't seem that sad to me…" *at a time when she's seeking emotional support and connection*, she will feel rejected because you rejected how she felt.)

To connect with her emotionally:

1) You DO NOT have to make yourself feel what she's feeling.

2) You can acknowledge how she appears to be feeling. Ex: "Sounds like you feel pretty hurt by this."

3) Listen without trying to fix the problem.

4) Ask more questions about what's upsetting her. Ask how she feels or what she thinks about this or that aspect of it.

Pay Attention to her likes, dislikes, skills, passions, and sense of humor. You don't have to ask her a million questions—you'll hear her say, "I love this," or, "I hate that." Watch her face and body language for when she lights up about something. What makes her smile or laugh the most? Take mental notes of these times. Make your actions speak to those things. For example, suggest a funny movie to watch together that you think has her sense of humor. If you've heard her say she likes Mexican food, take her to a new Mexican restaurant you heard about.

Be her protector – If you notice something you think may be a threat to her wellbeing that she doesn't seem to see, respectfully speak up about it.

Don't hide your vulnerabilities.

Don't try too hard to impress her. Try to be the best version of yourself you can be. And if that's not enough for her, you probably don't want that relationship.

Stick to your values. Don't lie about your values or preferences to "win her approval."

Culture

1. Cultural expectations

Whether you realize it or not, general beliefs of the society you live in can seep into your subconscious. You may not even know where any of your ideas about how men and women should be originally

came from. And you may not have ever stopped to consider how much sense these ideas make, either.

Our society can give us false ideas of what a "good" way for our partner to act is.

We have a lot of ideas on how men should be and how women should be. We have ideas in our heads not just about the opposite sex, but about our own. Some women think men *should* be strong and not express their emotions. Some men think women *should* be naturally good at being nurturing. Some women think women *should* not speak up if it's gonna rock the boat; some men think that men *should* never look at other women if they're in a relationship. A lot of these ideas our culture instills in us are not true.

2. The feminist mindset

A major problem in today's relationships is an attitude some women assume toward men that is directly linked to our culture's feminist movement. When the feminist movement started, it was about women being strong and capable and being acknowledged for that. They wanted to be treated as equals. As the feminist movement grew, our culture began to not just accept but cheer on women who showed men up and put them down—even if those men didn't mistreat women in any way. There is a difference between celebrating a strong, confident woman and celebrating a woman who is disrespectful to men. Women don't necessarily realize they're being as rude and cold as they are. They grew up believing that's the way they *should* be treating men. They grew up believing that men can take it. Or even that it's good for them. Knowing what we now know about how important feeling respected is to men, can you see how a woman acting disrespectfully can start the Crazy Cycle in a relationship?

Another misconception some women have that creates problems in relationships is that because men don't express their emotions as freely, they don't feel the emotions as strongly. Women treat men like they can handle anything—cold words and remarks, hurtful, rejecting body language and tone of voice. And women are particularly good at finding words that cut like a knife when they want to.

We don't need to prove it to you. If you are a human being living in this century, you probably watch movies, TV shows, listen to music with lyrics, read books, magazines, or social media, or witness people interacting with the opposite sex. You'll have no shortage of examples of the dynamics we're talking about, but here's a few of my personal examples:

a) I saw a video done as an experiment to show how onlookers reacted to an aggressive argument depending on the gender, made by people who want to raise awareness of male victims of domestic abuse. It was filmed at a London park with a hidden camera, and the couple having the "argument" were actors. When the "boyfriend" becomes aggressive with his "girlfriend," the onlookers rush to help, and one shouts, "Oi, mate, what's wrong with you?" Someone speaks with the man, telling him if he keeps it up, someone will call the cops, and a woman tells the "girlfriend," "You don't have to put up with this, hun."

The experiment was then conducted with the same actors but with the roles reversed (the woman was the aggressor). No one attempted to help the man. Instead, onlookers watched, and some laughed.

If you look around, you'll see how people think it's acceptable to treat women verses how they think it's acceptable to treat men.

b) I see this dynamic play out in movies all the time: The couple or love interests in the movie both do things that hurt each other. Sometimes the guy starts it. And sometimes the girl starts it. But almost *every* time, I see the guy is the one who has to beg forgiveness, make up to her, and make things right. And often, we also see she still gives him a hard time, WHILE he's trying to fix things! Why our society teaches females they don't need to be accountable for treating men badly is an answer I don't have.

3. The Demands on Men

There are jokes about it because it's often true: Women often want a lot more from men to be satisfied in their relationships than men want from women. Men are usually content if their girl treats them well, wants to do stuff with them, is generally a fun personality to be around, and makes them feel wanted. Women, on the other hand, often want their man to be a romantic lover, a strong knight in shining armor, their supportive best friend, their therapist, and their personal cheerleader.

Besides any expectation from men's partners, they face society's pressure. If you don't spoil your girl on Valentine's Day, you're a cheap bastard. (Are women expected to spoil men on Valentine's Day?) You're also a cheap bastard if you don't pay the bill for dinner. You're always supposed to do what she wants, even if it means ignoring what you want. Heard the saying "happy wife happy life"? That means keep your wife happy so that you can be happy. (Is there a saying suggesting women should keep their husbands happy to be happy themselves? Not anymore! People would say that's old-school and sexist. Yet, they don't see that the tables have turned in the opposite direction now, and everyone's okay with it.) Have you ever noticed people you know and strangers alike giving you (if you're the male partner) a hard time

for stupid little things like: you didn't hold the door for her, you let her carry more groceries than you, you're not cooking dinner for her...? We have experienced this. Not once do I recall someone giving me a hard time for not doing what I'm "supposed" to do as a partner or lover. Why? Because that would be sexist. Women are basically immune to criticism from guys, while the popular thing for everyone to do (not just women!) is give men shit.

Summary

What you want to remember:

1) Most men and women do have several defining differences.

2) In relationships, these differences don't get us into as much trouble as does the fact that we ignore our differences instead of respecting them.

3) Different brain function and other biological attributes cause us to communicate differently, love differently, and have different motives for our actions.

4) Most men's primary need in relationships is to be respected. Most women's is to feel loved.

5) If we want to stay out of crazy cycles and get our needs met, we must not "punish" our partner by withholding our love or respect if we think they withheld it from us.

6) Women typically want more from men in relationships than men want from women.

7) Society teaches us how men "should" be and how women "should" be. Following this thinking can and will destroy your relationship.

8) In our society, it's acceptable for women to be physically, mentally, and emotionally abusive toward men.

9) Men have more societal pressure on them than do women to be a good lover/partner/husband.

Chapter Nine

CONFLICT RESOLUTION

"For all the brilliant technology humans have invented and all the scientific discoveries we have made, we can still be pretty dumb. We think we have to fight against the people who care about us most, and act out against threats we make up in our heads."

– Mandie Bigelow

If couples fight a lot and are not good at resolving conflicts in a productive manner, the risk is that one person or the other may decide that the relationship isn't worth being unhappy that much of the time and call it quits. Depending on the attitudes and demeanor with which couples fight, they may end up hurting each other to the point that they feel resentment toward each other. They'll shut down and close off from each other for emotional self-protection, and the resentment they feel will leave no room for love or appreciation.

If you really want to understand conflicts and learn how to handle them, you'll love this concept from the book *The Celestine Prophecy*, by James Redfield (an adventure story about spiritual awakening and conscious evolution). When our book was in its

early days of conception, we knew we wanted to include this concept.

The book describes a set of different behavior methods people use to get energy from each other, which the author refers to as *Control Dramas.* The word "drama" means the particular behavior patterns we act out, like scenes in a movie or a play, over and over throughout our lives.

> *"...we humans seek to outwit and control each other not just because of some tangible goal in the outside world that we're trying to achieve, but because of a lift we get psychologically. This is the reason we see so many irrational conflicts in the world both at the individual level and the level of nations."*

> – James Redfield, *The Celestine Prophecy*

The book explains how energy makes up the entire universe, including ourselves. And scientists such as Einstein have proved it. This energy is referred to by many different names, including God, Spirit, Love, Source, or universal energy.

At birth, this energy flows through and within us. We are connected with everything. But when we grow up, we develop judgments, fears, and doubts, and more and more, we find ourselves feeling cut off—desperate to feel that blissful connection again.

In our attempts to feel better, we try to get other people to give us *their* energy. When we make someone else pay attention to us, energy (literally) streams from them *to* us. We mistakenly believe that getting energy from others is the *only way we can get it.* We don't realize we can get it ourselves, much less *how.*

"When love first happens, the individuals are giving each other energy unconsciously and both people feel buoyant and elated. That's the incredible high we call being 'in love.' Unfortunately, once they expect this feeling to come from another person, they cut themselves off from the energy in the universe and begin to rely even more on the energy from each other—only now there doesn't seem to be enough and so they stop giving each other energy and fall back into their dramas in an attempt to control each other and force the other's energy their way."

– James Redfield, *The Celestine Prophecy*

It's easy to see dramas acted out in intimate relationships. One drama triggers the other's drama, and thus, the tug-of-war for energy ensues. Relationships running on control-drama-power are exhausting and difficult to sustain.

"…Everyone manipulates for energy either aggressively, directly forcing people to pay attention to them, or passively, playing on people's sympathy or curiosity to gain attention."

Here are the four different types of control dramas. The book classifies them into passive dramas and aggressive dramas. Here, they range from the most passive (the Poor Me) to the most aggressive (the Intimidator):

The Passive Control Dramas

1. Poor Me

Those who use the Poor Me drama get your energy by attempting to make you feel bad for them, or feel guilty, so that you will do what they want.

2. Aloof

Those who use the Aloof drama get your energy by closing up and going into their shells, so that you have to poke, prod, and question to get them to talk.

The Aggressive Control Dramas

3. Interrogator

Interrogators get energy and take control by questioning and judging. They make you feel defensive and like you owe them a good explanation for everything they ask about. They question and judge you, even for things that seem insignificant.

4. Intimidator

Intimidators get energy and take control by use of fear. They may threaten you with anything from bodily harm to the loss of their friendship, to "or else."

Warning

You'll easily see what dramas those closest to you use, but the biggest pitfall is only seeing dramas in others and not in yourself. It takes self-awareness, and frankly, more balls, to admit to your own drama, but this is where real growth happens. I think the second biggest pitfall is always blaming others for causing your control drama. *It doesn't matter who started it!* This thinking is childish and bad for your relationship's health. What's the best thing you can do? Focus on how to stop the cycle, not whose fault it is.

What's My Drama?

First, look to your childhood and family of origin.

According to *The Celestine Prophecy*, we developed our main control drama in childhood to counter the control dramas our parents or guardians used. The behavior patterns became habit, and even after we grew up and left home, we continued to use the same control dramas in all our other relationships. Most of us use one main drama, but we may switch between others depending on our situation and/or who we're interacting with. Our main drama is whichever one seemed to work best for us on our family members.

Which Control Drama Creates Which

An Interrogator creates an Aloof.

An Aloof creates an Interrogator.

An Intimidator creates a Poor Me,

and if that doesn't work, an Intimidator creates another Intimidator.

The book didn't seem clear on what drama a Poor Me creates, but I imagine it would create another Poor Me, or possibly an Aloof.

How Does This Work?

Ask yourself, for example: Did your dad often seem critical, like you couldn't do anything right? Did he ask you lots of questions then find something wrong with your answers? If so, his main drama was an Interrogator. You likely became Aloof— not wanting to give him too much information to spare yourself from criticism.

Did your dad seem distant? Closed up like a clam? Was it a rare treat to hear a story from his past, or offer up any ideas or opinions? If so, his main drama was Aloof, and you likely felt you had to

poke and pry to get him to open up and give you attention—becoming an Interrogator yourself.

Did your mom often complain about what wasn't going well in her life? Did she often make you feel guilty for the problems you were causing her with your messiness, noisiness, or forgetfulness? If so, her main drama was a Poor Me. Maybe you learned to have competitions over whose life is worse, or you became Aloof in an attempt to distance yourself emotionally.

Did your mom often yell and threaten you? Did you feel nervous around her? Did you fear for your safety? If so, her main drama was an Intimidator. To get the energy to come back your way, you acted out the Poor Me. If that went unnoticed by her, then you became an Intimidator as well.

How to Stop a Control Drama Energy Battle

Don't participate

A control drama energy battle can only continue if both parties are participating. If one person doesn't fall into the corresponding drama when the other person acts out theirs, the cycle cannot continue. If you can notice when your control drama is taking over, jump on that opportunity to direct your behavior toward a more productive route. Or, you may be aware of the dramas of those closest to you. When you notice them falling into it, you'll be prepared for yours to kick in and you can put a stop to it.

Name the drama

Another way to stop an energy battle is to name the drama that's being used on you. This works because the dramas operate on a

subconscious level, so if you bring them up to the surface of consciousness, they cease to work.

For example, when someone uses the Intimidator and threatens you, you might try saying, "What are you angry about?" If someone plays Aloof, you might try saying, "Why are you being so vague?" If they play a Poor Me, you might say, "Why do you feel the need to make me feel bad for you?"

Other Points

Fighting vs. Conflict

A conflict is when you and your partner's ideas, beliefs, or values oppose one another. You need to make decisions about how to proceed in life together, and you will inevitably run into them. Often, couples fight when there's a conflict, but they don't have to. You can have a conflict without having a fight.

Don't look here to stop having conflicts. Although fighting is no fun, it's normal and in most cases unavoidable to fight sometimes. You may find ways to decrease the *number* of fights you have, and the *severity* of the fights. But as long as you are two separate people, you will have conflicts. Conflicts do not have to turn into fights. We have resolved *many* conflicts peacefully without name-calling, yelling, throwing things, pouting, stomping, or door-slamming.

Arguments Are Not Bad

Arguments don't necessarily mean your relationship is in trouble. They *could* mean that, especially if you're having the same ones over and over. You and your partner may be spending more time being miserable than being happy together. However, there are

some things to consider. 1: Sometimes, you're going through a low point. It would be in our best interest to try not to project meaning onto things. We may think that because we're going through a low point, it *means* things will only get worse. We may think it *means* that things won't change. We don't know these things. Our alien may be sabotaging us with these fears.

The way we're wired for survival makes the stressful and upsetting times more vivid in our memory and the times where things go smoothly more forgettable for most of us. So, sometimes, we think we're arguing a lot more of the time than we actually are. We may be drawing false conclusions.

Arguments between couples happen if both parties voice their opinions.

Couples in healthy relationships argue sometimes. It's not in healthy relationships that couples never argue; it's in *un*healthy ones. The only way a couple wouldn't argue is if 1) they each had all the same ideas, values, beliefs, and opinions, 2) one of them (or both) wouldn't consistently stand up for their values and beliefs. For example, if one party always gave in to what their partner wanted, kept their mouth shut when their opinion conflicted, *or* they took turns doing this.

With all our talk about honesty, transparency, communication, and integrity in this book, how good of an idea do you think we'd say it is to not argue in your relationship?

Arguments can make hidden issues visible before they become bigger issues.

Sometimes, when we're arguing about one thing, we start bringing up other things we're upset about. When we're already upset, we

may tend to be more brutally honest about our feelings than at times when we're calm. We didn't realize before that this past upset had anything to do with our current upset until we started arguing. Or, we had swept the past upset under the rug and tried to forget about it, but were reminded of it due to either our current emotional state, the subject of our argument, or both. We may start to discover more past upsets we didn't think were a big deal that all connect to a larger theme of something we're struggling with.

View arguments with our relationship's motto: There are no problems—only opportunities to learn and grow.

If you can remember to look for what you can learn or how you can benefit from the argument, you're mind goes into constructive problem-solving mode instead of attack-and-retaliation mode.

And remember that your state of mind directly impacts your physiology. Less fearful state of mind = calmer body, which = clearer, thorough, and creative thinking.

Other Strategies We Use to Decrease Arguments

Listening

Most of us suck at listening. Here's a real-life example I heard the other day (names changed). John said: "Where's Tommy?" Lily replied: "Tommy's hungry." Is it just me, or is "Tommy's hungry" not an answer to "Where's Tommy"?

Pay attention to yourself.

Pay attention to your alien. Try not to let his voice get in the way of hearing your partner. Try to just listen. Stop arguing what your partner is saying in your head while you listen.

Pay attention to your partner.

If your partner wants to talk with you, stop what you're doing if you can so that you can engage with them. If you keep your attention on something else and barely acknowledge that your partner is talking to you, your partner may feel what they have to say is not as important as what you're doing.

Listen to your partner when they talk to you. Listen with the intention of understanding them, their situation, or their feelings. Show them that their feelings, opinions, and wants matter by acknowledging that you hear what your partner expresses to you. Don't interrupt. Don't make your stuff more important than theirs. Reflect on your attitude and word choice when communicating.

If you don't think you're a good listener, you can learn. Here's what not to do:

Roadblocks to Listening

1. Minimizing the situation or feelings as your partner perceives them

2. Telling your partner what they should or shouldn't be doing or feeling

3. Ignoring them

4. Listening for a little while until something they say reminds you of your own story, which you then begin to tell

It may be helpful to ask if your partner is seeking to vent and feel heard, or if they are seeking advice. Giving one when your partner seeks another can feel extremely frustrating. (List how each

roadblock can influence your partner to feel, and how each can be perceived.)

Another way you can be a better listener is to ask questions and keep an open mind. This may not seem like listening, but asking questions to get the fullest scope of what your partner is saying to you will help make sure you understand your partner's message.

Don't automatically rule out the idea that you may be wrong—or at least partly wrong. Or that your partner may have a good point.

Treat your partner the way you want to be treated.

Would you enjoy it if your partner kept interrupting you when you talked? Or rolled their eyes at everything you said? Or never tried to understand your perspective? Most likely not. So, don't do it to your partner. Listen respectfully, *even if* you don't agree.

Don't Make Assumptions

When you stop communicating and assume beliefs, you give up your freedom. You become a prisoner of your mind.

Here are the things I try to keep in mind:

Be patient. Put off being upset or acting out about something until you've gotten all the facts.

Ask questions to see if your perception is the truth: "Honey, is it true that you made other plans when you knew we had a date that night or did you just forget?"

By jumping to conclusions, you could make a fool of yourself and create unnecessary drama.

Empathy

"Empathy is connecting with the emotion that someone is experiencing, not the event or circumstance."

– Brene Brown

Humans experience ALL the same emotions. It doesn't matter what culture you were raised in, what race you are, or your age. We don't all necessarily feel the same feelings in similar situations, but pick any emotion and we have all felt it at some point in our lives. Even if you can't relate to having that emotion from a similar experience, you have felt the emotion at some point in a different situation. It is a way we can relate to ANYONE, no matter how different we feel they are from us.

Language Accuracy

Language accuracy can decrease conflicts and make communication so much easier. By using more accurate language, you can also train your mind to find solutions easier.

Most of us don't realize how inaccurate our language actually is.

Common examples of inaccurate language to avoid:

a) Exaggerating

If you have a habit of exaggerating, your partner will not know the difference when you are and when you're not. You may not get the attention, support, or help from your partner if they don't know when to take you seriously.

b) Promises

We make promises with the best of intentions. We want our partner to feel safe, like they can count on us, and to feel reassured of things they may fear. Most of us don't think about why making promises could cause trouble. 1) Even if we don't mess up on our end, there are plenty of things outside our control that may prevent us from keeping the promise. 2) Circumstances may change, and although we *could* still keep the promise, it may not be in line with our and/or our partner's best interests anymore. 3) If we want our partner to be able to count on us, and count on our word, making promises that you can't keep undermines that. There are some things you can honestly promise, however. You can promise to try, and you can promise to do your best. When we wrote our wedding vows, we did not write lists of promises to each other on purpose. The promises we did make were to do our best to love, and to work to keep our relationship strong.

c) Finite words

Words such as "Always," "Never," and "Can't" are almost always inaccurate, unless you use them with *almost, seems like, feels like,* or *right now.* If we use finite language consistently, we teach our brain to believe what we say. This affects us emotionally and psychologically. Saying, "I'm always broke," feels a lot worse than saying, "I'm broke right now." The first statement doesn't allow our mind to entertain possible positive change, and the second statement does. Our beliefs shape our reality. Even if we don't like being broke, if we *believe* "I am always broke," we will unconsciously take action to align our reality with our beliefs. We will make choices that continue to keep us broke. Well-known motivational speaker, author, and life coach Anthony Robbins agrees. He said, "The way we communicate with others and with ourselves ultimately determines the quality of our lives." Note the "*and with ourselves*" part.

d) Disempowering words

Words such as "Should," "Shouldn't," "Should Have," "Couldn't," or "Can't" are disempowering because they place the credit or responsibility on someone or something outside ourselves. Instead, saying more accurately "won't," "don't want to," or "I wish I had," you're owning your choices and taking responsibility for your actions and desires.

Teaching your mind and your partner that you are not responsible for your choices teaches you to be a slave to your surroundings and others and not believe in yourself. It will be harder for your partner to trust that they can count on you and will likely cause many conflicts.

Imagine you are saying (or say out loud), "I *shouldn't* have overbooked myself today so that we get no time together." Now, "I *wish* I hadn't overbooked myself today so that we get no time together." The first you may find feels something like you're punishing yourself. The second, at least to me, does not. The second is expressing regret for your choices, but not in a way that makes you feel wrong or like you failed.

Now, imagine (or say out loud), "I *can't* keep you happy." vs. "I *want* to keep you happy, but I don't know how."

"I *couldn't* ever do that," vs. "I *won't* do that because_____."

"I *should* go to that fund raiser," vs. "I don't *want* to go to that fund raiser."

e) Emotional vs. Factual

Often, if we *feel* like something, we say it like a *fact*. For example, "I'll NEVER be able to have a normal relationship." This is how

we feel. It is not necessarily true. We can't see the future, so we don't know if this statement is true or not. Saying this, we are lying to ourselves. To be accurate and develop mental habits that help us rather than hinder us, we can say instead, "I FEEL like I'll never have a normal relationship." All we have to do is add "feel."

Things we use often to make our language more accurate:

1) "I feel…"

2) "A part of me feels____, while another part of me feels____." (When conflicted)

3) "right now"

4) "seems like"

5) "almost"

6) "sometimes"

Things that get in the way of accurate language:

1) Stress (when there's a lot on our mind, we're not paying as good of attention to ourselves)

2) Emotions (we say feelings as if they were facts)

3) When we want to appear a certain way to our partner, or make our partner feel a certain way

4) Not paying attention to yourself for whatever reason

Communicating from love during a conflict of needs

1.   You have to say what you want while respecting your partner's needs.

2. Do it from a neutral place—try to view the situation objectively.

3. Don't self-sacrifice. You will end up feeling resentful.

4. Don't manipulate or try to force your partner to give in to you.

Self-Sacrificing: The Cost of Not Speaking Up

You can be honest when your partner asks you a question, and that is a good thing. But if you are the kind of person who grew up believing that your value was determined by what other's thought of you, you have to make sure you don't sweep your desires under the rug to avoid the possibility of conflict. There's nothing wrong with occasionally setting what you want aside because you think that's best for the team in the situation, but if you do this consistently, you become a slave. And you do it ALL to yourself.

I have some experience with this kind of belief system I'm referring to, because I would consider myself one of those people who have adopted it. Your main goal when you're a kid is to make sure those close to you are happy at all costs. You see that when you act kind, you are thought of as a loving, sweet person. You feel good about yourself. You continue to be as good as you can so that you can keep feeling valued. You learn that you feel best if you don't argue with the general consensus, so you don't speak up if you think what you want might be rejected. You think that if people like you, then you are accepted, loved, and valued. You want to avoid anything that could make you feel wrong, rejected, worthless, or uncaring.

The pattern continues in romantic relationships. Your partner will say things like, "Why do you always take things personally?" or, "I don't feel like I can ever be upset without you making it about

you!" This is because you can perceive just about anything to be your fault. You said or did something that triggered something in your partner. You blame yourself for their being upset, even if you couldn't have known or it was a complete accident. Your beliefs attack: "I'm not good enough," "I failed my partner," "I'm so stupid, I should have seen that…"

You get into this state, and how well do you think you'll be able to be there for your partner? THEY were upset, you had an opportunity to give them love, clarity, and strength, but you end up making them drag you out of feeling sorry for yourself. Beating yourself up is actually a technique used to get love and attention when you feel bad. You feel bad because you believe the lie that if your partner isn't happy, it's your fault—you are not enough—then you try to "get" the confirmation that you ARE loved, you ARE good enough, from your partner to feel good again.

If you try to avoid triggering your partner, here's what it may cost you:

1. Your happiness.

2. Your partner's happiness.

3. Your relationship.

Your happiness, because you are not listening to your heart. You keep on affirming to yourself that your wants, thoughts, and feelings don't matter, that you don't deserve respect, and you don't deserve to have the things you desire. Talk about ingraining the unworthy belief!

You will also not appreciate being happy if you spend your effort on avoiding being *un*happy. It may appear that you do avoid

outward conflict in the moment when you don't speak up, but you create inner conflict, which manifests outwardly between you and your partner anyway.

Your partner's happiness, because do you really think your partner can be happy if you aren't? And if your partner struggles with not-enough syndrome, never being able to make you happy is a sure way to trigger it.

If neither of you are happy, why would you want to be in a relationship?

Speaking Up vs. Getting What You Want

Voicing what you want with consistency does not always equal getting what you want. You might think you would be happier always getting what you want, but if you want to be part of a team, it should be balanced. How do you think your partner would feel always giving in? Resentful? And how happy and connected do you think you could feel toward them? Not too good? Thought so.

It's good for both of you to express what you like, what you want, think, and feel to each other. But you have to be okay with not getting what you want every time you express it. The point of you both getting what you want out there is to have an easier time working together to come up with a plan you BOTH determine is best for BOTH of you. Depending on the situation, one of you may need to compromise due to time or money, but you could decide together to try and make that thing happen with the next opportunity you have. (Which may mean the other partner has to compromise *their* desires at *that* time.)

When you don't speak up, you are also taking away something that is extremely valuable to your partner: the ability to make you

smile. Your partner LOVES to see you happy! This is not an unusual phenomenon in a healthy relationship! YOU hold the keys. How do you expect your partner to know how to help you be happy if you don't tell them what you want? Like the classic line goes, "You can't expect me to be a mind reader!"

Order of best to worst ways to communicate (conflicts or emotionally charged subjects)

a. In person

Communication isn't just what we say, it's *how* we say it, what tone of voice, how loud or soft, what kind of posture, where we're looking, what we're doing with our hands, the spaces we leave in *between* our words, our sighs, our expressions. This is why in person is the best if we want the best chance of understanding each other.

b. Skype

Through Skype or other video chat, we still can hear and see to some extent all of the above. However, technology can glitch or we can have trouble connecting, which can add to pre-existing frustration.

c. Over the phone

We can still hear everything, but we lose any visual cues of communication.

d. AVOID, IF AT ALL POSSIBLE: Text, Facebook messenger, or other chat systems

When in an argument, or discussing emotionally charged subjects, don't expect resolution to be easy. It's so easy to misunderstand

just the written word. Not to mention that autocorrect may be "correcting" our words, making our sentences have a completely different meaning.

The Missing Ingredient in Conflict Resolution

It's not what your partner *did* that upset you; it's what you *thought about* what your partner did that upset you. Pinpoint the thought your partner triggered, not just the feeling. It's not as simple as, "You did this, and I felt this," it's, "You did this, I thought this ABOUT what you did, and so I felt this."

Summary

Conflicts are caused by a battle for energy, and we can stop them by naming the drama our partner is using and resisting acting out our own. Conflicts are inevitable, and they do not necessarily mean our relationship is in trouble. We can prevent some unnecessary conflict if we remember to use accurate and specific language, avoid making promises we can't keep, speak up for our wants and needs, avoid expectations, and listen to our partner without judging, minimizing, making it about us, or trying to "fix it" (unless they want us to). When trying to resolve a conflict, it's best to talk in person due to visual cues and tone of voice helping us understand each other; it's really not a good idea to communicate via text or messaging apps, due to easily misunderstanding things said.

Chapter Ten

HANDLING EMOTIONS

"The hero and the coward both feel the same thing.. But the hero uses his fear, projects it onto his opponent, while the coward runs. It's the same thing, fear, but it's what you do with it that matters."

– Cus D'amato

Have you ever exploded in anger at your partner and said things or done things you wished you hadn't? Of course, you have—we all have. But it doesn't have to be this way. The trick is to deal with whatever is bothering you *before* your frustration builds up to the point where you lose control.

Here is the diagram Tobey invented for visualizing your range of emotional states—from completely calm and clear headed to exploding in anger. He calls it your Emotional Response Continuum. "Satori," in the oval on the left, is the state when your mind is not cluttered with thoughts; you are completely present and therefore at peace emotionally. "Exploding," in the jagged bubble on the right, is the state when your mind is overwhelmed with thoughts that make you angry, hurt, or scared. Therefore, your emotional state is chaotic, and your actions are irrational and out of control. The arrow moving toward the right in between the two vertical lines represents the entire range of emotional states in between Satori and Exploding. It also represents the time it takes us to go between these two extremes.

If something upsets us and we don't deal with it (by talking with our partner, reasoning it out ourselves, etc.), we let it fester in our minds. We get more and more upset about it, and eventually, we explode. Alternately, lots of small irritations can pile up, and eventually, if not dealt with, one tiny irritation will tip us over the edge.

Either way, if we pay attention, and admit to ourselves when we're upset, we'll have multiple opportunities to escape off our path of destruction and return to a more clear-headed state where we can work things out rationally. (This is just another way of representing The Sphere diagram when referring to the alien.)

The curved lines coming off the arrow and returning further back on the line or to Satori represent all the opportunities you have to do something about your issue before you explode. That means writing about it, talking to your partner, breathing, taking a walk, or anything you find that helps you calm down so you can think more clearly and start finding solutions. And no, none of these options include ignoring your feelings and hoping they go away. You also need to remember you don't need to return to Satori to solve your problem. It would be ludicrous to think you had to return to a completely peaceful state of mind when you're already upset. Anywhere closer to it from where you are is better than ignoring your distressing thoughts and feelings and eventually exploding.

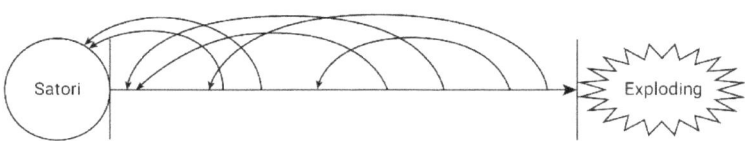

We Each Have Our Things

We each have our "things"—our particular alien programs that, when triggered, can really set us off. Mine, for example, is the "I'm not good enough" alien program. In my experience...

1. Learning to handle your emotions is not about getting rid of your "things."

2. It's about learning how to handle your things when they come up, how to grow from them, and how to live with them.

3. The more stressed you are, the more prone you are to your things coming up.

4. Whatever your things are, and whatever your partner's things are, they seem miraculously matched to set each other's off and perpetuate a cycle of one person's stuff triggering the other person's stuff. This has been observed and documented by many relationship experts, psychologists, and therapists.

5. Clues to Your Triggers:

1. What do you feel you stand for? What are your values?

2. What quality in yourself do you view as very important? For me, it's being caring. For Tobey, it's having integrity to himself— being the person he wants to be regardless of life's challenges or his emotions.

3. If you could see more of a specific trait in humanity, what would it be?

When Our Top Self-Value Appears Threatened

What upsets us the most is when we perceive we are being accused of not being a way that we are that we place high value on. For instance, I get upset when I perceive that Tobey is feeling like I don't care about him, or that I'm not acting caring, because I actually am a caring person, and I place high value on this trait. Likewise, it upsets him if I accuse him of not acting in a way that aligns with the person he wants to be, which is a trait he is very good at and places high value on.

We know that things become more challenging when strong emotions come up during a conflict with our partner. We know about how the alien causes our ability to think rationally and make good decisions to diminish. We learned how the alien is behind

these strong feelings and how to bust him. Here are some additional tips and perspectives for handling strong emotions:

Stop trying to change how you feel.

Emotions change on their own. Emotions are like clouds in the sky. You are the sky, and the emotions are the clouds. Emotions come and go, and yet the sky remains. You are not your emotions, just as the sky is not the clouds. Remember, you are not stuck with this feeling forever—you will be happy again. Sometimes, we can change our emotional state, but sometimes, trying to change our emotional state not only wastes our energy but may also make us feel worse. Instead, focus on your behavior. How are you interacting with your partner? On a scale of how bad things seem, you have the power to make things go from a five to a ten quickly, depending on how you choose to act.

"It's not about controlling what you feel; it's about choosing how you act."

– Tobey Bigelow

We can feel one way, yet choose to act another.

It *is possible* to feel like yelling and name calling but not do those things. We may tell ourselves we can't—that it's too hard—but that's BS. People do it all the time. Think of a woman working a customer service job. Maybe her dog dies that morning before she goes to work. She feels like crying, but she holds it together because she wants to keep her job.

It's not *easy,* but we can do it too. And the ability to do so when in an argument with our partner can be the difference between finding a way back to common ground or destroying the relationship

entirely. We may need to think before we act—about how our next action may affect the future of our relationship. We can ask ourselves, "Is what I'm about to do worth it?" We can act with a higher purpose in mind rather than satisfying our urge to lash out at our partner because of how we feel in that moment.

Try not to take things personally.

The more hurtful your partner acts, the more they're hurting.

One thing most of us do is to take things our partner says too personally. Everything we hear sounds like a threat, an insult, or an attack on our character. Sometimes, we know we're taking things too personally and making the argument worse, but we don't know how to stop.

If you both understand the importance of communication and do your best to live by it, not only will you be communicating what you do like, but what you don't like as well. When your partner brings up something you did that bothered them, it can be difficult to handle if you struggle with the failure complex. Sometimes, it won't matter how or even what exactly they communicate to you. They may only be expressing how they feel, not blaming you, but if YOU are blaming you, then it can seem like your partner is blaming you as well. If you're vulnerable to an alien attack at that moment for any reason, he can go off on a tangent about you not being good enough, smart enough, about you being a failure at life and with your relationship—what's wrong with you? And on and on. You can get so wrapped up in your feelings caused by believing your alien's shit that you forget the situation is temporary. You forget that your partner is upset with what you DID, not with YOU. And just because they are not happy in that moment doesn't mean they are not happy with you, you in your entirety, you all the time.

This makes perfect sense, seeing as your partner chose to be in a relationship with you of their own free will.

If you are listening to your partner's complaint or feelings, the place you're in mentally, emotionally, or physically has a giant impact on the message you hear from your partner and how you handle that message.

There is a difference between taking out your frustration with other things on your partner and being frustrated with other things and therefore having a lower tolerance for some of your partner's less pleasant behaviors. The difference is the first is making your feelings your partner's fault. The second is not. It's not beneficial to accuse your partner of "taking stuff out" on you without being certain they are. You only send your partner the message that they are not treating you well because something else is upsetting them.

When you feel you're taking things too personally, here are the different scenarios that may be occurring:

a) Your partner may be acting in a way most people would consider hurtful (with or without being aware of it).

b) Your partner may *not* be acting hurtful, yet you still *perceive* that they are.

c) Your partner is acting a little bit hurtful, but how you react emotionally to it seems out of proportion. (Note: How you react emotionally *can* be out of proportion to your partner's words or actions. But how you react emotionally will *always* match what you *think* is going on or what you're *afraid* is going on or might happen.)

If you DO want your partner hearing your side, there is NO POINT in getting defensive.

Your defensiveness can easily appear as attacking your partner, then they feel the need to be defensive, you feel attacked, and you both get caught in a loop where your sole purpose is to defend and attack and you'll completely lose sight of the real problem and how you might solve it. Would you feel any interest in hearing your partner's perspective *while* you're also feeling the need to defend yourself? No? Your partner won't feel like listening to you while trying to defend him or herself either.

Remember, your partner has fears too. Fear can come across as anger or hostility. They may have a fear of the relationship ending, whether or not to trust, or a fear of being misjudged by you.

Don't verbally attack your partner

No relationship is conflict free, so you need to be able to work stuff out in a way that doesn't turn you into enemies.

Your partner won't want to hear you or help you. We know no good comes of saying mean things, but we still do it sometimes. We feel hurt, so we want to hurt back. We think this will make us feel better, but it does not.

How to use your feeling as a guidance system to resolve issues

1. You and your partner describe your feelings.

What's your worst fear about the subject? For example, "I'm afraid you'll leave me for someone smarter and prettier than me." Or, "I'm afraid I'll never be able to measure up to the person you want me to be."

2. Turn your feelings into basic statements.

When feeling something strong, focus solely on that feeling and try to put words to it. Ask yourself, what am I feeling? Don't second-guess or judge what you get. You don't usually get something logical or scientific or mature. What you're doing is tapping into the part of you that some aptly refer to as your inner child, so if you get something that sounds like what you might hear a child say, that's probably exactly how you feel. You might get, "Nobody wants me!" Or, "I'll never be good at this!" Or, "Nobody cares about me!"

3. Ask yourself what that statement means to you.

What are you afraid the consequences of your statement(s) are? If you want to make sure you're on the right track, your answer will probably be one of these things: 1) You *have* something that you're afraid to *lose*, 2) You *want* something that you're afraid you'll never *have*, or 3) You have something you *don't want* that you're afraid you'll always have.

These are all about lack, and are all the alien.

"Negative" emotions aren't "bad"

Intimate relationships can trigger all sorts of "negative" emotions to flare up from time to time. The other person is not actually *causing* us to feel the way we do, our *thoughts about* them are. Even so, knowing this doesn't stop us from sometimes feeling completely overwhelmed.

Many people are discovering the power of positive thinking and are using affirmations to counter negative emotions. Affirmations do have their place; however, I firmly believe that our "negative"

emotions are not actually bad. I think they are there to bring our attention to something that we need to see. The more painful the feeling, the more beautiful the gift is beneath—waiting to be uncovered.

When we try to force ourselves to be positive, we are not honoring our feelings. For me, this only makes things worse. Feelings have only one ambition in life, and that is to be felt. When I face my feelings head on with an attitude of, *Yes, I really do feel scared. I accept this feeling and I accept myself. I know my true self is okay, and this is just a feeling.*

Bust the alien. Work with your partner to disprove the false fears.

Contagious Emotions

Keep in mind that the emotion behind what we chose to talk about affects our partner as well. Everyone has mirror neurons, so on a physiological level, we can't help synchronizing to our partner. Whether we try to or not, we will take on, so to speak, some stress if our partner is stressed. Or if we are feeling down, our partner can feel dragged down to some degree as well.

From an energetic perspective, this is also true. But this goes beyond affecting each other when we are in each other's presence or talking on the phone, to affecting each other no matter where we are.

It's not just a negative state that we infect each other with; we can infect each other with a positive mood as well. We can lift each other up just by being happy ourselves.

Summary

Try to work out what's bothering you before your emotions get out of hand. If you wait until you're exploding, it will be hard to think or behave rationally or resolve the issue(s) with your partner. Handling strong emotions is not about getting rid of them. Your feelings are a guidance system, so allow them to help you. Your emotions do not have to dictate your actions. Our emotions don't cause problems—our actions do. Strong emotions come up when you and your partner "trigger" each other, especially when you perceive a threat to your most-valued character or personality traits in yourself. If you both value communication, you can expect to be discussing behaviors and quirks you're not so fond of. If you're learning how to not take things personally, remember that your emotional response has more to do with you than it does with whatever your partner said or did. Be aware that emotions are contagious—we often pick up what our partner is feeling, and our partner picks up how we're feeling.

Chapter Eleven

GETTING UP WHEN YOU FALL

"Those that believe they can and those that believe they can't are both right."

– Henry Ford

Notice this chapter isn't called "Getting Up *If* You Fall," it's called "Getting Up *When* You Fall." When we take learning how to improve our relationship seriously, we take our growth seriously; when we grow, we *will* fall. We will take some steps backward. We are not, overall, *going* backward. But at times, it certainly feels like we are. The saying "three steps forward and two steps back" is often true. Also, we often take our biggest leaps forward in growth after our largest setbacks.

The Line of Growth

Changing our old ways of thinking and behaving that aren't serving us is challenging. But why do we sometimes feel like we are going backward on our personal growth journey instead of shooting ahead from all our new insights and knowledge?

The horizontal line below with a vertical line at each end represents a segment from your infinite line of growth. The curving and

looping arrow moving from left to right is you on your personal growth journey over time—whether that means improving your self-awareness, your self-esteem, the way you handle adversity, or the way you communicate.

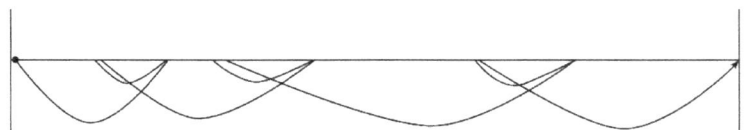

You'll notice after every period of growth, the arrow takes a little loop backward before moving forward again. Not only does this happen to *everyone,* but it is *impossible* to keep growing *without* having any setbacks. Since setbacks are inevitable, you might as well accept that they'll happen. Not only that, but our setbacks can actually teach us what we need to learn to move beyond our furthest reach on the line of growth. Overall, we are growing more than we are backsliding. We only doubt this sometimes because we can't see the big picture.

Here is your line of growth again, this time showing what happens when we fight against our setbacks. The bold arrows going backward show how handling setbacks poorly makes you backslide even further than your previous setback. For example, after one of your normal setbacks shown above, you notice that you're not functioning at the place you were before. You might notice some of your old habits coming back that you had been doing better with. You get frustrated with yourself, you start listening to your alien talk about how you suck, growth is impossible, how you'll never get better at such and such, etc.

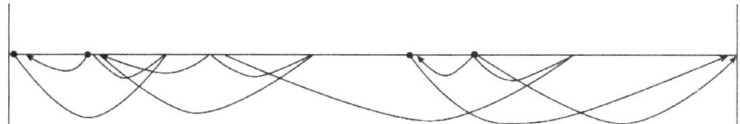

Anytime you are backsliding further after a setback, you can stop it by noticing what's going on, remembering that your alien is telling you lies, and being kinder and more accepting of yourself and where you're at. Once you do, you'll be back on the line of growth moving forward again. You also don't have to struggle forward at the same pace as you did before; you can leap forward, skipping over previously trodden ground.

Since "falls" are inevitable, here is our list of things we've found helpful for getting back up again:

List of Strategies

1.   Dress up and go on a nice date with your partner.

2.   Observe your thoughts. What are your deepest, most painful ones? Bring your awareness to them and find out if they're true. (Bust your alien.)

3.   Find a high-energy group activity to take part in like a sport or dancing.

4.   Ask for help or guidance, from a higher power you believe in, your higher self, or someone you trust.

5. Let go of trying to "fix" your state. Accept that you're down. Remind yourself that feelings always pass.

6. Go be in nature or at least outside. Find beauty.

7. Exercise or do something physically demanding.

8. Keep your eyes open for opportunities to help others, or even just offer a compliment to make someone's day.

9. Write down what's bothering you—everything. Then, write down the most uplifting, comforting things you could imagine hearing someone else saying to you.

10. Meditate, practice breathing, or just bring your awareness into your body and observe what you feel.

11. Do The Work, especially if you feel anger toward someone else.

12. Hold a Power Posture for a minute or two.

(Power posing is the idea that holding confident or powerful postures creates hormonal changes, which leads to us feeling more powerful and confident. It's a psychology hypothesis that was introduced in 2010 by Dana Carney, Amy Cuddy, and Andy Yap (wikipedia.com).)

13. Read a favorite book.

14. Clean, or organize a space that has become cluttered.

15. Plan a trip or adventure.

16. Go somewhere you haven't been or try something you haven't done.

17. Work on a project you've been putting off or haven't prioritized.

18. Watch a funny movie or TV show with a friend or your partner.

19. Use the OODA Loop.

The OODA Loop is a decision-making tool created by military strategist John Boyd. OODA is an acronym for Observe, Orient, Decide, Act. Designed to help individuals and organizations succeed/win in chaotic environments, you can use it to help you find clarity. Observe your surroundings, but you can also observe your thoughts and emotions. Orient yourself by analyzing everything you've learned from your previous experiences, and find any incongruencies in your beliefs about what's happening now. Decide: use this information to make a decision. Act: follow through on your decision with action. Repeat the OODA once your actions have created change.

20. Put things in perspective.

It could always be worse. Think about how many people are in much more challenging situations than you. This is not to make you feel guilty or bad somehow, but to see the accuracy of your perspective that you should be miserable.

Make a list of any of these ideas you like, or any others you know that make you feel good, and keep it in your wallet. Pick one and do it.

Accepting after a high

After a good day, or after you have felt like you are making progress, or have had a good perspective, you will sooner or later have a day where you feel a little down, a little like nothing has

really changed. Or you can even have a drastic shift in perspective and feel miserable.

The point is that it is hard to accept where you are immediately after a high. But if you don't accept where you are, and try to make yourself feel how you know you just felt the day before, you will only be fighting yourself and will quickly get in an even worse place.

Accept where you are FIRST. Then do whatever you know works to change your perspective.

Takeaway

When you're consciously growing, at times you will feel as if you slip backward in your progress. Remember that OVERALL, you are still moving forward.

Chapter Twelve

KEEP DATING FOREVER

You know what you did and how you acted when you were dating. Keep doing it! Don't stop just because you're married, have kids, or life gets in the way! Dating doesn't have to take time, money, or tons of effort. But you have to *make the time*—don't *wait for the time*.

Whether you're still dating, engaged, newlyweds, or have been married twenty years, *keep dating each other!* Find things you both enjoy doing, and if you get stuck in the same routine for a long time, put effort into doing something out of the ordinary. Try new foods, new activities, and go see new places. You may discover a passion you never knew you had.

If you're still early into the dating phase, you might notice how you both naturally take turns lifting each other up. You're thinking of each other, and want to express that you care and value each other. If you've been together for longer, you may find you have lost the desire and motivation to keep up with this give-and-take love game. But that doesn't mean you can't pick it up again, and consciously do the type of little thoughtful gestures and surprises you did for each other in the beginning to get the ball moving again. It may feel like work at first, but it won't stay that way.

Six awesome tips to help you keep dating forever:

Thoughtfulness

Pay attention to your partner's values and honor them with your actions. Notice the things they want or need but won't buy for themselves, and gift one of those things for the next special occasion (Tobey has always done this for me!). Offer to do something for your partner that you know they don't like doing themselves.

The little things count

You've probably heard this saying before, "It's the little things that count." Or, "Actions speak louder than words." While you probably don't want love expressed only through actions, these are valid points. And we are here as more proof saying that the small, everyday actions that show we care and respect our partner are invaluable.

The unexpected

Surprise each other with small gestures of love and playfulness

Quality time

Time together without distractions beyond what you're engaged in

Humor

My husband makes me laugh—a lot. He has all these different personalities and voices that just come out at random. I never know who I'm going to be sitting next to from one moment to the next. He acts silly because it makes me laugh. If I stopped laughing, he told me, he'd stop doing it. But it's great. The more laughter you

have and light-hearted you keep your attitude in your relationship, the easier it is to deal with the stress and challenges of everyday life.

You don't have to be good at making your partner laugh. Bring humor into your lives however you can. Watch comedy or something you both find funny together, play games that make you laugh, or hang out with friends whom you mutually have a good time with.

Appreciation

Look for and discuss the positive interactions in your relationship

We did a Facebook quiz together where we took turns telling each other things we like about the other's character, things we admire, appreciate, and respect.

How to Express Appreciation Meaningfully

1.   Think of something your partner did or said or a quality in them that makes you feel good

2.   Tell them what specific action or quality you appreciate

3.   Tell them WHY that matters to you—how it affects you for the better. Does it make you feel safe? Cared about? More confident?

Summary

Don't forget to *make time* to have fun together. Don't let life "get in the way." Find common interests, find things that make you laugh or make each other laugh, change things up if you get stuck in ruts, pay attention to what the other likes, do the little things—

they mean a LOT—and express appreciation for each other meaningfully.

Key Takeaways

If you remember nothing else…

1. Our goal is to move away from acting out unconscious destructive patterns in our relationships and to living and acting in our relationships on purpose.

2. You need to be willing to look at yourself objectively and admit the part you're playing in your relationship's problems. Before we can change anything for the better, we need to be aware of what we think, say, and do.

3. Communicating as openly and honestly as we can is one of our relationship's building blocks.

4. Knowing that happiness comes from within ourselves, and not falling victim to the belief that we "get" our love and happiness from our partner is one of our relationship's building blocks. We must feel we are complete—or good enough—by ourselves, not like we need our partner to "complete us."

5. Trying our best to see the challenges in our relationship as opportunities instead of problems is one of our relationship's building blocks.

6. Being aware that the fears of our mind are often lies, that they can sabotage our relationship if we believe them, is one of our relationship's building blocks.

7. Letting the idea that we are a team guide our actions and decisions is one of our relationship's building blocks.

8. Taking into consideration and respecting the fact that men and women think, act, and communicate differently and have different values and motives is one of our relationship's building blocks.

9. Conflicts are caused by a battle for energy, and we can stop them by naming the drama our partner is using and resisting acting out our own. We can prevent some unnecessary conflict if we remember to use accurate language, avoid expectations, speak up for our wants/needs, listen without getting defensive, refrain from verbally attacking each other, and avoid making promises we can't guarantee.

10. Try to work out what's bothering you before your emotions get out of hand. Remember, it's not about controlling how you feel—it's about controlling how you act.

11. When you're consciously growing, at times you will feel as if you slip backward in your progress. Remember that *overall,* you are still moving forward.

12. Don't forget to *make time* to have fun together. Don't let life "get in the way." Find common interests, find things that make you laugh or make each other laugh, change things up if you get stuck in ruts, pay attention to what the other likes, do the little things—they mean a LOT—and express appreciation for each other meaningfully.

Thank you for reading! We hope you can put this information to good use. We wish you all the love and happiness you can stand!

– Tobey and Mandie

ACKNOWLEDGMENTS

We would like to thank both of our families for their support and enthusiasm for this book, and also our friends and social media followers for their dedication and encouragement.

We want to thank our editor Paisley Prophet, our book designer Waqar Nadeem, Morgan Clasper for the author bios and book blurb, and Bipin Rupadiya for doing our interior diagrams. You all did amazing work!

We want to thank our beta readers for their feedback; my mom, Sandy Littell and sister, April Littell.

We very much appreciate those of you who gave financial contributions to help make publishing this book possible; Sandy Littell, Morven Allen, Chris Salmon, Breanne Lee Kydd, and Sarah King.

Finally, I want to thank Tobey for the many, many discussions about the concepts in this book, for being the mastermind behind this book's construction, and for motivating me time and time again when I'd put the book on the back burner.

www.ingramcontent.com/pod-product-compliance
Lightning Source LLC
Chambersburg PA
CBHW051215120626
46547CB00013B/1369